$10.25

Adirondack
Album BY BARNEY FOWLER

An unusual view of New York State's famous North Country by a veteran reporter-photographer, containing with text more than 300 illustrations of past and present.

5556-1-7

To those who said, and in no uncertain terms: "Stop talking and start writing!"

Contents

The author is not partial to hard-to-read small type. Nor is he partial to photographs compressed to sizes where details are not adequately portrayed.

As a result, this book has been designed for easy reading and its pages are eight-and-one-half by eleven inches for better display of photographs. The type used is 11 pt. Press Roman medium, and captions are in 10 pt. Press Roman italics.

The paper used in this volume is Finch Opaque, cream white in color, vellum finish, chosen to eliminate glare and for quality in photo reproduction. It is a New York State product and is manufactured by the Finch Pruyn Paper Co., of Glens Falls.

Preface

My friend Barney Fowler and I were up in Newcomb in the heartland of the Adirondacks during the height of the Gooley Dam controversy. Construction of the Gooley Dam across the Upper Hudson was proposed by the City of New York back in the late 1960's as a water supply measure. The proposed dam did not materialize. Had it done so, two thirds of the hamlet of Newcomb would have been flooded. As we drove with Town Supervisor Lilburn Yandon, looking at the various areas of the town that would be affected, we passed an old cemetery that would be under water.

Barney asked the driver to stop and hopped out with his camera while the rest of us visited in the car. In a few minutes he returned with a satisfied smile on his face. The next day his feature article in The Times-Union read: "Newcomb Man Drowned — Twice!" Barney had found and photographed a headstone in that graveyard of a woodsman of olden days who had been drowned in one of the annual Hudson River log drives back in the 1800's. I've often thought to myself that there's the hallmark of a top newspaperman — to be able to find and tell the really interesting stories in, around and behind the news.

Even though he is widely known as a newspaper columnist and feature writer-photographer on general interest themes, Barney Fowler has never ignored his basic love for the outdoors and in this, his first book, that fact is evident.

In his career with The Times-Union and the Schenectady Union-Star Barney estimates he has produced well over 15,000 columns, at least 2,000 features and thousands of news photographs, with subject matter reaching into such widely diversified fields as crime, politics, rackets, business, human interest, police and other facets of urban existence. But emphasized often has been the outdoor scene and in 1967 the New York State Conservation Council, composed of 350,000 members, took cognizance of this fact. In cooperation with the National Wildlife Federation and the Sears-Roebuck Foundation, the Council presented him with its highest award in the writing field, naming him "Conservation Communicator of the Year."

He has had other honors as well; one from the New York State Forest Rangers Chapter of the Civil Service Employes Association for his efforts in bettering working conditions and salaries. In 1970 the prestigious Lake Champlain Committee of more than 2,000 members from New York State and Vermont cited him for his efforts in helping institute the holding tank law for boats using New York waters. Within this time span he also was a national prize winner in the annual Scripps-Howard Newspapers Conservation Awards Contest, competing with outdoor experts throughout the United States.

In another field in which he has crusaded, Barney has been cited by the 3,000-member PBA of the New York State Police, not once, but twice, in 1959 and again in October, 1973.

He has covered every beat in the newspaper field; has combined purposeful photography with writing. At age 15, for instance, while Assistant Sports Editor of the Union-Star, he was the first to disclose publicly in the

1930's the creeping paralysis of the imported water chestnut weed in state waters. The battle against this exotic, Asiatic growth, is still going on. Its origin is described in this book.

Many years of moving about the Adirondacks has resulted in thousands of negatives. Barney's skill is not within the so-called "artistic" field. It rests in photographic realism. While he appreciates the sheer beauty of mist rising from a mountain pond in early morning, he'd much rather center his camera's eye on the face of a bear awakened from its Winter sleep in the Raquette Lake section. This does not mean his photos are not artistic in a natural sense but the fact remains they are essentially news photos with centers of interest. The series of photos showing a raccoon robbing a bird's nest is indicative of this.

It is from this negative file he has drawn material for this book. Some photos have seen publication before, in Outdoor Life, Yankee Magazine, in the New York News, New York Times, the old Herald Tribune, Denver Post, as well as on United Press International and Associated Press wire services. The first photo he ever sold nationally, as a matter of interest, was of a frog sitting on a thumb tack! The amphibian, incidentally, was from a fresh hatch in the vicinity of Ticonderoga. For a few years he varied his free lancing diet as a feature writer on outdoor subjects and personalities for Pacific Stars and Stripes as well as for publications in England, Scotland and France.

The man himself? He is a newspaperman, first and foremost. He is a public speaker who has addressed thousands of groups. For recreation in weaponry he is an archer, although he does possess firearms for target practice and, at one time, was a safety instructor for the National Rifle Association.

His approach to the Adirondacks is not the usual one. He stalks with the analytical eye of a newsman. His bark is not worse than his bite; both are equal. He states opinions whether he is bucking a politician, a sportsman's club or a corporation. He is not noted for pulling punches and many a toe has been stomped upon. By the same token, he cheerfully concedes his have received the same treatment.

With others, including this writer, for instance, he opposed Laurence Rockefeller's idea of turning the Adirondacks into a National Park. In the face of organized state political and business pressures, he fought for holding tanks against macerator-chlorinators for boats using state waters. His crusade against snowmobiles is almost an obsession, has encouraged near apoplexy to many — yet in the Essex County Cancer Crusade in 1973 he did something he vowed never to do. He rode and drove a snowmobile. But it cost sponsors $1 a foot and more than $2,000 was raised in this phase of the overall cancer campaign.

If he personally is opinionated, which he admits, so are his writings. He is against the bounty system on any wildlife, including timber rattlesnakes and brush wolves.

He sanctions restricted use on what he terms over-used mountain trails. He favors limiting use of power boats on heavily used lakes and favors damming the Hudson at Luzerne, thus creating a new lake from that community northward to Warrensburg. He favors outlawing power craft on many lakes and rivers. He has disagreed publicly with some policies of the New York State Conservation Council, with many of the State Department of Environmental Conservation, and with some voiced by the Adirondack Park Association, of which organization at one time he was a vice-president. He stands foursquare behind the controversial Adirondack Park Agency and supports closing off of wilderness areas to all forms of motorized traffic, including airplanes and, of course, snowmobiles.

Barney is not an armchair writer. He has climbed peaks, hiked the flatlands, canoed rivers and lakes. He is familiar with the Allagash in Maine, but the New York Adirondack wilderness is his first love. Once, for the sake of a story, he lived for three days in the Oswegatchie River section, armed only with a bow, arrows and a knife. The live-primitively theme was so finely honed even his campfires were made by friction — using the bow and spindle method! He is a student of animal life, having raised bear and panther cubs, raccoons, deer and a variety of other wildlife. Many of the resulting photos are to be seen in later chapters.

Included is an astonishing variety of pictorial stories. Barney has studied the Rogers Rangers from their arrival at Fort William Henry at Lake George in 1755 to their departure. He has also included a chapter on three famous boats which sailed Lake Champlain, the Vermont, considered the world's second successful steamboat; the Philadelphia, one of the first American Naval vessels constructed under the verbal whiplash of Benedict Arnold at Whitehall (now in the Smithsonian Institution in Washington, D.C.) and, finally, he has followed the dry-land career of the last side wheeler on Lake Champlain, the Ticonderoga, as it was hauled overland to its incongrous, waterless sanctuary at Shelburne Museum, Shelburne, Vt.

The story of the famous swim of Diane Struble, first to conquer the length of Lake George, deserves more than casual mention; Barney was among the first to recognize her extraordinary swimming ability, was among those encouraging her in her successful attempt from Ticonderoga to Lake George Village in 1958.

The newspaperman's approach is ever evident. When Barney heard of the "stone baby," a lithopedian carried by a Herkimer County woman within her body for a half century, he dug up 19th century medical records to prove the yarn.

When he heard of a virgin white pine at the famous Pack Forest north of Warrensburg called the "Grandmother's Tree" he dug up the background to that story as well. It, too, is contained in this volume.

Photos of rattlesnake hunting by Elijah (Willie) Clark on Tongue Mt. were obtained while Barney hunted the reptiles with Clark, who sought income from the bounties which existed then. Barney was a friend of the late Fred Streever, of Northwest Bay, Lake George, author, foxhound breeder, poet, designer of primitive American homes, and an early hunter of the Adirondack coyotes or "brush wolves." Noah John Rondeau, the famous hermit, was another friend; in this volume is the last photo made of Rondeau as he passed his final moments of life at Placid Memorial Hospital. Jacques Suzanne, who raised timber wolves and malemutes near Lake Placid, and who died in the Essex County Infirmary at Whallonsburg, was another friend. Still another was the late John S. Apperson, who created a legal storm in his attempt to have Lake George water levels of today lowered to the ones existing during French and Indian War days. In the 1930's Barney helped organize and promote the first snow train from Albany to North Creek. He is considered a pioneer by the ski fraternity of New York State.

You will find a chapter devoted to historic forts of the Lake George-Lake Champlain region. Barney was present with his camera when the first shovelful of earth was turned at Fort William Henry when that fort's reconstruction was begun. He was also present when the oldest unexploded mortar shell on the North American continent was found on the site. He was instrumental in obtaining the services of an official U.S. Army bomb squad to deactivate the shell. He has been present at further excavations at Fort William Henry, as well as on Rogers Island in the Hudson off Fort Edward's shores. He has watched Fort Ticonderoga expand and has hunted artifacts on its extensive grounds.

His newsman's fervor has led him into crusades other than those mentioned. His chapter on desecration of the North Country by vandals and litterbugs is a devastating indictment of those people who don't care.

For nearly three years, Barney was a controversial commentator over WGY, relinquishing that medium to devote creative efforts elsewhere. This book is one of those efforts; Barney terms it Volume One of a series. Hopefully there will be many more Adirondack books to come from his pen and camera.

It is a worthwhile effort, timeless in interest, a chapter on the Adirondacks worthy of any bookshelf; in a way, it is a guide for those who have not yet become acquainted with some of the many faces of the Northern Mountains — the same faces which make the Adirondacks so unique.

William M. Roden, Trout Lake, N.Y.

A wilderness lodge in the late 1800's. From a photo by G.H. Rison, New York State Forest Commission Report, 1894.

P.F. Loope, former Executive Secretary of the Adirondack Mountain Club unloading a canoe near Griffin Rapids on the famed Oswegatchie River, St. Lawrence County. In the 1870's and 1880's this was one of the areas prowled by George Muir, the State's top timber wolf and panther bounty hunter.

Introduction

There is substantial reason for this volume. It is to offer something new under the Adirondack sun, specifically, a photo-journalism tour into the dramatic past, present and whenever possible, a look into the crystal ball of the future of these ancient peaks, valleys and flatlands. It is not an encyclopedic adventure of facts and figures but a montage of memories, many on film, and comments of a newspaperman who has been in love with the area as long as he has roamed it with camera and notebook.

The French explorer, Jacques Cartier, is considered by many to have been the first to have swept his gaze over the vast Adirondack wilderness in 1536, only 44 years after Indians greeted Columbus and only 30 years after the death of that inspired explorer. If this is true, and there is no reason to disbelieve, Cartier had uninterrupted visibility. Smog, which covers some sections of the mountains today, had not been invented. No mountain top weather station existed in those days to tell what is told today by personnel of the Atmospheric Sciences and Research Center station atop 4,867 foot high Whiteface Mt., that a portion of the North Country receives air pollutants from as far distant as America's Southwest.

There are many who credit Cartier with first glance, but Samuel de Champlain with first penetration. In 1609 Champlain moved southward from the St. Lawrence River to a spot near the present location of Fort Ticonderoga and there fought his famous battle with the Iroquois, a battle which made the Iroquois Confederacy the deadly, relentless enemy of the French.

It might be noted here that the same battle, which involved the Mohawks of the Iroquois, led to a somewhat unusual promise at a later date. The Mohawks were anthropophagous, but ritualistically so; they cannibalized those portions of enemies which they thought would transfer similar strength into their own bodies. This chilling gastronomic tendency was non-discriminatory and the Dutch at Albany finally met in solemn conclave with the Mohawks, extracting from them the promise they would no longer "roast" any Dutchmen, but would concentrate their gourmet activities upon the French.

Explorative prongs were developing fast in 1609, for in that same year Henry Hudson was busy sailing his Halfmoon up the Hudson River to the site of what is now Albany. Lake George was known to exist only through Indian accounts. The Jesuit missionary, Isaac Jogues, was probably the first European to see that spring-fed body of water in 1642 as he passed through the area as a tortured and bound captive of the Mohawks. Later, on May 30, 1646, he returned to Canada as an emissary of peace and this time, standing upright instead of resting flat in a canoe, he "discovered" Lake George. In all probablility he stood near what is now referred to as the "million dollar beach" and he named the lake "Lac Du St. Sacrament," Lake of the Blessed Sacrament.

It wasn't until 1755 that Sir William Johnson, in charge of Indian affairs for the British, fully aware of what flattery will do for a man's position in life, renamed the lake in honor of the British King.

All this, of course, occurred on the eastern fringe of the Adirondacks; the deep interior was still comparatively unknown save to native Indian populations, and not too much is known of this early occupation today. Such is under study by the Adirondack Museum at Blue Mt. Lake.

Mountains without names are called many names before one sticks in the public mind. A 1570 map called the northern area of New York State "Avacal." Ho-de-no-sau-nee-ga was the Iroquoian designation for the wilderness. The Peruvian Mountains was still another; this was bestowed by early French because of South American memories and suspected treasure; reference to the North Country in this fashion is made in an 1813 Gazeteer owned by this writer.

There were other names. One was Mountains of St. Marthe. Still another, and more interesting, was Corlaer's Mountains. The latter referred to Arent Van Curler, Dutch founder of Schenectady, who supposedly lost his life when he canoe overturned while he was on a mission to visit Gov. De Tracy of Canada in 1667. This tragedy occurred, some accounts say, when Van Curler (referred to as Corlaer by Indians) made a decided derogatory gesture at a rock sacred to Indians paddling his canoe.

The rock is a few miles north of Crown Point. Specifically, it is said, he thumbed his posterior at it. After he was swallowed by Lake Champlain and Indian friends sadly reported that fact, his widow continued her existence by running a pub in the Old Stockade area of Schenectady.

Twenty-three years after Van Curler's death, the French and Indian allies swept down on snowshoes during the winter of 1690, and destroyed Schenectady. Such was the political scene in those days.

The Adirondacks were not called by that name until 1837. The designation has remained, although upstate New York is still referred to by many simply as the North Country. As a matter of fact, the Upper Hudson at one time was known as the North River. So tombstones over the graves of drowned lumberjacks reveal.

The Adirondacks have often been called mountains of mystery. Perhaps this was true in the early days. It is not today, with millions annually visiting the six million acre Park in which the mountains exist. There are few spots where man has not set his hunting, fishing or hiking boot, his privately chartered airplane, his devastating, raucous and annoying snowmobile, his trail bike. And there are comparatively few lakes and ponds which have not felt the impact of his boating and, more importantly, the pollution of his outboards. The latter is a subject of which the public is just beginning to become aware. A chapter will be devoted to that environmental tragedy and how its solution has been stymied.

In some areas, such as in the Mt. Marcy region, so many have hiked trails that portions of mountain sides literally are being eroded and ecological damage is feared. New peaks of garbage are being erected by na-

Tombstone of victim, Byron A. Alden, drowned in the North River (Upper Hudson) in 1872. Grave is located in Newcomb.

ture lovers and there is talk of limitation of number of climbers, which I doubt will ever happen. A few years ago a team which climbed the mountain to remove some of the junk left thereon, estimated at least 14 tons rested topside. In all probability the tonnage has gone up, despite pleas from conservationists to "carry out what you carry in."

Much of this situation can be attributed to the fact that new roads, new superhighways, bring in a different breed of "outdoorsman," many of them strictly city sportsmen who, having read of the wonders of the Adirondacks, come to enjoy them, mangle them, and leave their signs behind — in the form of litter and hieroglyphics sprayed on once untouched cliff walls. It is not surprising to this writer that the famous King Philips Spring, for instance, just off the Northway alongside the Keene Valley road, was closed because of possible hazards to health. Its temporary death was foreordained when the Northway (I-87) came into being and brought additional hordes into the region. Passersby have used the spring area as a public toilet.

Despite the increased invasion of humanity, there are still unnamed bodies of water. This was proved when under the public land use plan of the Adirondack Park Agency, the State Department of Environmental Conservation closed some 700 lakes and ponds to all motorized traffic in the Summer of 1973, a move incidentally, which brought howls of protest from some. Some ponds were identified in this closure only by longitude and latitude; if once they had names, these were never recorded, never accepted, long forgotten.

If mystery exists today it is spacial in scope; exists partially in the fact that anorthosite, a rock found in the Whiteface Mt. area, is similar to that found by American astronauts who walked and drove on the moon. There is little mystery left in minerals; the Adirondacks produce titanium at the mines at Tahawus; once produced high quality iron ore from 3,000-foot deep shafts at Mineville; talc and lead are mined in the Northwestern section and some of the finest garnet in the world can be found at the Barton Mines at North Creek. There have been efforts to find gold and silver but these have failed. Graphite was once mined near The Hague, but cheaper, imported materials forced the closing of these shafts.

Over many years, after reading dozens of books on the area, I came to the conclusion that while words flow easily — and millions have — the pictorial drama and background has not received what I consider proper emphasis in actual consolidation. This is not to minimize Seneca Ray Stoddard's nostalgic photos of the past, nor those fine photos of any photographer of the present. Untold thousands of excellent pictures exist in many hands, in many museums, in many attics; more are being taken every day in all seasons, yet these are scattered. Nowhere have I come across any publication in which the photo theme dominates. I have tried to rectify the situation.

At the same time, nowhere have I come across any volume which presents the general mountain area from a modern newspaperman's standpoint, and there indeed is a difference between the views of a newsman and a chronicler. If I call the Adirondacks my "beat" I must attribute this to Richard Lawrence of Elizabethtown, Chairman of the Adirondack Park Agency.

Two or three years before this controversial (but necessary) agency came into being through action of Governor Nelson A. Rockefeller and the New York State Legislature to protect the Adirondacks from uncontrolled development such as suffered by neighboring Vermont, Dick Lawrence suggested I write a story for the popular Adirondack Life Magazine, tops in its field.

"What about?" was my natural question.

"About how you cover the region," he replied. "How you learn of your stories. How you dig them up. How you choose them. Treat the Adirondacks as your beat."

I never did get around to the magazine story but the idea took hold, rooted and sprouted into this book.

While dominately pictorial, it also contains provocative stories I have come across during some 40 years of traveling the country. Some examples:

Historically, the most famous band of deep-forest warriors of early America during the French and Indian War period of the mid 1700's was without question the scouts called Rogers Rangers. This corps of hard-bitten, tomahawk and scalping knife wielding maurauders was born in the eastern Adirondacks, over Fort William Henry way at Lake George. In material written about its remarkable founder, Robert Rogers, I have found few illustrations, fanciful or otherwise. Galileo may have perfected the telescope but nobody had as yet gotten around to inventing the camera. In modern versions of Rogers' own journals, I found no pictures of consequence.

Yet today there is physical evidence of this man's impact upon the Lake George-Lake Champlain region, in museums at Fort William Henry and Fort Ticonderoga. I am indebted to both for use of their facilities and permission to photograph items. These are presented. There are many imaginative, strikingly well done paintings of the famous Rangers; some of these also are printed. I am indebted to the Glens Falls Insurance Company for its permission to reprint paintings from its excellent collection. I am equally grateful to the ownership of the Holiday Inn at Lake George for permission to use Ranger pastels, created by one of the finest artists in the North Country, Charles Hawley of Lake George.

Scattered physical artifacts and paintings present an unorganized overall picture; joined together the scene grows more vivid. Lest the impact of Rogers Rangers be underestimated, I might point out his rules of guerrilla warfare exist as the foundation for rules used today by the military forces of the United States, and were widely utilized not only during World War Two in the Pacific but in the Korean and Vietnam Wars as well.

The year 1958 is less than two decades in the past. But that was a year something extraordinary occurred at Lake George; the lake was conquered for the first time by a swimmer, Diane Struble. Is her story to remain buried in newspaper morgues and to be forgotten? Hers was a truly remarkable feat of endurance and courage; exhausting hours in the water, from Ticonderoga to Lake George Village, where a throng of 10,000 vociferous admirers acclaimed her triumph. There is no reason to bury that moment in memory alone.

In books, pamphlets, brochures by the dozens, perhaps hundreds, you will find mentioned the fact that once the Adirondacks furnished Europe with much of its furs. I don't believe completely the old saying that one picture is worth 10,000 words, but I do believe the copy of a ship's manifest of fur deliveries destined for Europe out of Albany in 1750 (photo contained in this chapter) recaptures far more dramatically than prose what the North Country and its trappers and hunters did produce to warm and adorn European bodies.

This is the ship's manifest of the "Nebuchadnezzar," showing furs shipped from the Adirondacks to Europe in 1750. The 58 "Musquash" refers to muskrat skins. Note "2 catts," which refer to panther hides. Shipment left Albany, destined for London, England. The Adirondacks proved a vast reservoir of animal hides of great variety for European markets. Original record owned by Mayor Erastus Corning, 2nd, Albany.

If you study famous hunters of the mountains, you will come across many names. Most, seemingly, are old time guides. They most assuredly deserve their place in the hall of hunting fame. But too little mentioned is George Muir. This unusual man came to my attention for the first time in a bulletin issued by the New York State Museum in 1899, unobtainable now but worth 15 cents in that year. George Muir didn't specialize in bears or deer. He was a bounty hunter; his economic meat were panthers and timber wolves.

He didn't kill the last panther (sometimes called the mountain lion, cougar or painter) in the Adirondacks; that distinction, if such it can be called, went to A.P. Flansburgh on Jan. 6, 1890. Flansburgh, hunting in the Town of Day, Saratoga County, collected the last bounty payment of $20 for a big cat punctured by his lead in this fringe area. But Flansburgh killed only one; Muir put 67 panthers into permanent pasture lands! That figure is astonishing when it is realized the bounty system of $20 per animal came into being in 1871 and between that year and 1890, bounties were paid on 107.

I have devoted space to animals long gone or believed to have been driven elsewhere. Space also is devoted to more common wildlife as it exists in the Adirondacks today.

Other aspects of the North Country have not been ignored. Bill Roden in his preface — for which I offer sincere thanks — has outlined many. I have tried not to make this a historical offering, but to tie history with the present; made the attempt to present current problems and in some cases their solutions. Geographically, this volume involves happenings and background within the so-called "blue line," which on maps shows the outline of the six million acre Adirondack Park. But at the same time I have included stories involving the fringe area, what I consider the Adirondack region. The influence, the stories within the park do not stop at specific boundaries, but spill over. To me, the Adirondack region starts at the Mohawk River, ends at the Canadian border. The eastern boundary is Lake Champlain. The western boundary ends west of the Old Forge area.

Much of my material has been obtained first hand. This, at times, has created conflicting accounts. For instance, one author said the Revolutionary War gondola, the Philadelphia, was found by grappling. The discoverer and owner himself, the late L. F. Hagglund, told me he found it looming as a mass in front of him as he walked the bottom of Lake Champlain in a hard-hat diving suit. Such differences, however, are relatively few and minor; the fact remains that in the case of the

Philly, the boat was found, salvaged and unfortunately for the new museum planned for New York State in Albany, it is now in possession of the Smithsonian Institution in Washington, D.C. I doubt if the Smithsonian ever will relinquish it for return to the state in which the craft was constructed.

The late Harold G. Veeder, former Schenectady and Albany realtor, whose genius sparked off the reconstruction of Fort William Henry, today a major attraction in the Lake George region of the Adirondacks.

Previously I said this volume is presented to offer something new under the Adirondack sun. There are, of course, other reasons. One might consider this an armchair escape into the richness of fond memories, to relive on paper. Another is because while the area offers no riches in gold or silver, it literally is a treasure trove of stories and photographic opportunity.

It might even open new facets to an old territory. As a youth, I camped overnight on the graves of men and never realized that skeletons were six feet under my sleeping bag until much later, in the early 1950's, when the reconstruction of Fort William Henry was begun by the late Harold G. Veeder, and archeologists disclosed that my old camping ground was the graveyard of possibly hundreds who had lived and died at the French and Indian Was fortress.

Still another reason is that while the Adirondacks may be more than a billion years old, leveled by wind, rain, snow and sleet, gouged by glaciers, they show change. This change is not physical, but socially and environmentally. Unless they are protected as they exist today, unless they get their own blanket type of security, they will lose their most valuable attraction, epitomized as a refuge for those sick and tired of city tensions.

I would like to believe that while much of the North Country is privately owned, there will be more of that land sold or deeded to the State for all of us to enjoy. I would like to believe that the visitor would wear two hats, one for city habits, one for the forested area; that the entire Adirondack Park and region be considered priceless, which it is; literally a gem to be guarded by all.

Which it should be.

W.L.Fowler

Goliaths in Green

LE MAJOR ROBERT ROGER
Commandant en Chef les Troupes Indiennes au Services des
Americains

Violence leaves its stark evidence in the deep wilderness.

Fragile bones of a cottontail may remain at the base of a tree, from whose heights they dropped as a hawk tore the creature apart. A handful of fur may remain along a deer trail where a whitetail was ambushed by a pack of dogs or brush wolves. On a vaster scale, thousands of trees may rest as flat as hair on a sodden wig, the result of tornadic winds touching upon their area.

Man leaves evidence as well.

"The bones of the victims remain yet unburied on the summit, and the curious are doubly compensated for their labor in ascending to view them, by an extensive prospect of the surrounding country."

So penned Horatio Gates Spafford, a Saratoga County newspaper publisher who was not only a distinguished member of the New York Historical Society but author of a Gazetteer of the State of New York published in 1813.

What Spafford described, however, was hardly the type of tourist attraction any Chamber of Commerce would publicize today in the northern Lake George region.

In actuality, it was an open graveyard located on what was known by early French as Mt. Pelee, later changed by the English to Rogers Rock. The "Rock" is a 1,000-foot slope of naked granite which dips precipitously into the waters of Lake George's western shore, south of Ticonderoga.

Spafford was describing what physically remained of one of the bloodiest confrontations of the French and Indian War, the famous "Battle on Snowshoes," fought in the deep snows of mid-March, 1758, between seven ranging companies commanded by Capt. Robert Rogers, and the French and their Canadian and Indian allies.

Brief though it is, the astonishing aspect of the historian's disclosure is that it was written a full 55 years after the savage battle!

Thus in a single sentence Spafford revealed the ultimate, shocking fate of an early British-American scouting force caught in an Adirondack ambush, a fate ghoulishly dramatized in succeeding years by an abandoned display of bleaching skeletons for tourist-climbers to view — along with, of course, the "compensation" of a superb panorama of Lake George far below.

No burial courtesies were extended to those warriors who fell under musket fire, tomahawks or knives; if skeletal remains of the fallen Rangers were visible to gaping tourists more than a half century after the battle there is little likelihood anyone save nature ever got around to covering them. Today, more than two centuries later, bones may exist for the unearthing. In all probability, curiosity seekers, being what they are and were, many of the remains probably were picked over as souvenirs. It is not an impossibility to contemplate that as you read this, there may be a Mt. Pelee skull adorning some recreation room mantle, staring somberly at raucous activities before it.

Few of the Rangers survived the holocaust on snow; of the 180 frontier fighters Rogers led, 125 were killed or listed in his own account as missing. French figures differ. Louis Antoine de Bougainville, aide-de-camp to the Marquis de Montcalm, brigadier general in command of regular French troops in Canada, in giving the French version, said the Iroquois, Nipissings and Abnakis "brought back 144 scalps and took seven prisoners." That would account for 151, a substantial portion of Rogers' force.

The French version of this historic battle is interesting and seldomly, it seems, brought out. Bougainville said the French "had two cadets wounded, a Canadian wounded, three Iroquois and a Nipissing killed, 18 Iroquois wounded, almost all severely, and an Abnaki, whose arm it was necessary to amputate." One assumes the French removed their wounded and deserted their dead, a not uncommon practice in wilderness conflicts miles from home base — in this case, Fort Carillon, now known as Fort Ticonderoga.

(The situation has a parallel of sorts. At Little Big Horn in Montana, 118 years later, the skeletal remains of Gen. George Custer's men lay on the surface for the curious to see and photograph. Eventually all of Custer's force of 264 men were buried. Rogers' men obviously received no such ceremonial attention.)

In the furious battle on Mt. Pelee, the hatchet, bayonet, tomahawk and scalping knife were used with

7

extraordinary skill and dispatch; both the French and the Rangers were surgical experts with the cutting tools of their trade. There was even time for torture; one Ranger, tied to a tree, was hacked to death.

Supposedly Rogers kept his hair by an ingenious method of escape from the hellish scene. Legend has it he snowshoed to the edge of the precipice facing the lake, dropped his haversack over the side and then, reversing himself on his snowshoes, walked down a gradual and nearby incline to the frozen lake below. Indians, coming upon the edge shortly thereafter and noting two sets of tracks leading to it, and observing the swath cut by the descending haversack, concluded Rogers and a companion had indeed made the daring descent. The Ranger commander makes no mention of such escape in his journals. The tale is a hard one to swallow.

In his report, Rogers said his men killed 150 of the enemy, wounded as many more. He also estimated the French strength at 700 — 600 of them Indians. The French account sets their total force at only 250, including 200 Sault St. Louis Iroquois. These were Indians converted by French Jesuit missionaries, and forgetting early hatreds engendered by Champlain in 1609, fought under French colors.

Such statistical differences are found frequently in historical records of battles long gone from memory. Whatever the totals, the event was a personal catastrophe for Rogers, even though it did not halt his elevation to major on April 6, less than a month later. The blow was to his pride; it was one of the few times in a lively and predatory career on the Lake George-Lake Champlain frontier that this noted bushranger ever ran into ambush. Usually it was the other way around. Had Rogers been given the 400 men he asked for, the results might have been different. Later, he said with obvious bitterness:

A J.L.G. Ferris portrayal of the bloody "Battle on Snowshoes" between Rogers Rangers and the French and Indians in March, 1758 at Rogers' Rock. Painting is used through courtesy of The Glens Falls Insurance Company, a member of the Continental Insurance Companies.

Pastel by Lake George Artist Charles Hawley, one of four depicting Rogers Rangers, owned by The Holiday Inn, Lake George.

"I will not pretend to determine what we should have done had we been 400 or more strong; but this I am obliged to say of those brave men who attended me (most of whom are no more) — both officers and soldiers in their respective stations behaved with uncommon resolution and courage. Nor do I know an instance during the whole action in which I can justly impeach the prudence or good conduct of any one of them."

Bitter words and justified. Rogers had asked for 400 men; had been turned down by Col. William Haviland at Fort Edward. Such snubs were not uncommon. The Ranger captain lived with them constantly. He was a tremendously gifted woodsman; probably six or more feet in height, which would have made him a giant in those days of small men; he was athletic; a savage wrestler and a born leader. Often he was frank to the point of bluntness. His reputation as a bold and brilliant fighter was outstanding. It was to be expected this lusty import from New Hampshire, unschooled in the niceties of imperious British leadership, would often run into differences of opinion with his commanding officers. Jealously is not confined in selection of its targets.

Rogers was, after all, only a New Englander in his early twenties, a natural leader it is true, but hardly a member of the inner circle of somewhat pompous British officers whose very lives at times depended upon his scouting skills. And, of course, his men, hard-bitten, hard-nosed frontiersmen from the New England states and the Mohawk Valley, reflected their commander. Their discipline, or what there was of it, was such that at Fort Edward they were bivouacked outside the fort, on what is known today as Rogers Island.

The island, several acres in extent and larger than in Colonial times because of dumpage of fill during the deepening of the Hudson, has been under archeological scrutiny during the past several years and the area has produced a considerable number of artifacts.

If the Rangers were kept out of Fort Edward, they also were considered too obstreperous to remain within the walls of Fort William Henry at Lake George. Here they also lived outside the fort. In both cases it was a wise move for both regular troops and Rangers. Fighting was common between the branches.

9

Additional pastels of Rogers Rangers at the Holiday Inn, Lake George. Artist Charles Hawley used Earl Bump, well known area political leader, as model in top panel, and Lake George Deputy Mayor and Police Commissioner Howard MacDonald for lower reproduction.

On Rogers Island, for instance, imposition of harsh British discipline on the Rangers brewed mutiny and in 1757, the British, following custom, set up a whipping post. Rangers were flogged with cat-o-nine-tails for a variety of reasons, including the theft of rum. They fought among themselves as well, and floggings were administered for these breaches of conduct. Regular soldiers fared no better. "Straggling" was considered an offense punishable by 100 lashes. One unfortunate soldier, tried at a general court martial and found guilty of theft, was sentenced to 1,000 lashes. Still another found guilty of what was termed "mutiny and insolent behavior" had his back torn apart by 500. Desertion meant instant death. Mercy, if it existed, was measured by the ounce.

The fiercely independent Rangers viewed whipping with almost as much undisguised horror as Indians viewed hanging.

"I was in mortal dread of the whipping," one said. "I felt I could not survive the shame of being trussed and lashed before men's eyes."

Yet this was the type of man who would subject himself to unbelievably harsh conditions in the wilderness of the mid 1700's, whose courage and cunning were such that he proved a figure of terror not only to the French but to their Indian allies as well! These, too, were the men who on their patrols formulated rules of scouting which even today constitute the basis for American military patrols. The rules tabulated by Rogers were used in the South Pacific during World War Two and in Korea and Vietnam; this America owes to Rogers.

On Dec. 6, 1757, the whipping post had aroused such resentment and stark hatred that a small mob of Rangers cut it to pieces with their hatchets. Rogers at the time was ill with malaria, a disease some believe he contracted in his Lake Champlain prowls. Col. Haviland, commanding Fort Edward, heard the uproar, ordered his regulars to quell it and suspects were clapped in the guardhouse. Two days later Rogers lifted himself from a sick bed to be present at the inquiry — which resulted in no action. The British, imperious though they were, had flashes of understandable lucidity; the watchdogs in greens were too valuable to beat into a sullen submission that might, on occasion, backfire.

The final panel in Artist Hawley's portrayal of Rogers Rangers, depicting a Ranger on patrol as Rogers and his group made their way northward toward ambush at Rogers Rock.

An astonishing archeological find on Rogers Island, Fort Edward, a vase of Chinese manufacture, showing the Biblical Wise Men. Vase was probably owned by a British officer stationed on the island. Found by Earl Stott, owner.

It becomes even more understandable that Rogers would be in conflict with British brass. His background in New Hampshire included a counterfeiting charge which faded when he volunteered to build the companies of scouts so badly needed. Rogers himself was unnerved by the charge and for good reason; the crime was punishable by slitting ears. He consistently pleaded his innocence but the shadow of the accusation followed him years after he became famous not only throughout America but Europe as well. The very realistic fact remains if there had been no desperate need for men of his abilities to counteract maurauding French terrorists, his ears might very well have been sliced and he would have become a New Hampshire rural nonenity, a village drunkard, years before he ac-

tually became notorious for that handicap. Rogers, despite military brilliance, died an impoverished drunkard at age 64, in all probability in alcoholic delirium, mumbling and at times shouting memories of his glory days on the New York frontier. He died alone. Few mourners appeared at his burial.

Rogers owed at least the beginning of his reputation to Sir William Johnson, who in 1755 was the British crown's appointee whose job it was to hold the allegiance of the Iroquois Confederacy to the overseas sovereign. The task was not easy. The French, as has been mentioned, already had converted some of the Mohawks to their own ranks. Rogers and Sir William met in 1755 during the period when Johnson reached military heights by defeating the French in the Battle of Lake George — and subsequently began construction of Fort William Henry. In time their temperaments struck sparks and the two became bitter enemies. The lust for land held by Sir William had much to do in the enmity. Rogers in 1761 petitioned for a grant of 25,000 acres on the west shore of Lake George, starting at what is now Lake George Village and continuing several miles northward. Sir William blocked the move indirectly by urging his Mohawk friends to protest. The substance of their complaint: The land was their ancient hunting grounds. Rogers did not get the grant.

Fort William Henry lived a brief existence, from 1755 to 1757, when it was burned and its garrison massacred by the French forces under Montcalm. During its existence and for a few years later, Rogers lived a spectacular life in the Adirondack region. His men were trained both at Fort William Henry and Fort Edward. No dummy weapons were used. Rangers learned to use knives by practicing with the real thing. Wrestling was perfected into an art and warfare with the tomahawk was part of the training. Skill in killing meant survival. No Ranger sought oblivion.

The French took little notice of early forays of the Rangers against Fort Ticonderoga. But as they became more adept at raiding, of capturing convoys and prisoners, they became a positive force in French thinking. The latter called them "forest runners." The Indians who had good reason, called Rogers "Wabo Madahondo," or "White Devil." For sheer ferocity, the Rangers have seldom been surpassed. They took few prisoners unless they were prizes sought.

In 1756 when their impact was first felt by the French, Rogers' men were at first thought to be small parties of Scottish Highlanders. This could have been prompted by the fact that part of the Ranger uniform — such as it was — included a long shirt, belted at the waist, plus a type of headgear resembling a flat Scottish bonnet. From a distance they appeared as soldiers in kilts.

This original impression was quickly dispelled. The Rangers were a breed apart. The hundreds of forays made by these green-clad master predators resulted in valuable information for the British; Fort Ticonderoga was in the process of completion and information on

Above: Diver surfacing from Lake George's depths with kettle once used by Rogers Rangers; utensil found off shore from Ranger camp.

Right: Hatchet found at Fort William Henry, used by Rangers. Note "I Speak" imprint.

French activity was sorely needed. Rogers and his men furnished it. No one else possibly could; the Rangers were seeing eye attack dogs with the power of speech and retaliation. The 32 miles between Ticonderoga and Fort William Henry were miles of total wilderness, almost without trails, literally a no-man's land. Rogers often used whaleboats on scouts. When the surface of Lake George was frozen his men often used ice skates. When snow shrouded the forest and sheathed the ice they used snowshoes.

Feats of the Rangers often bordered on the heroic. On one expedition Rogers' men rowed with muffled oars several miles north on Lake George, disembarked, carried heavy whaleboats up and over a ridge of mountains on the eastern shore separating Lake George from southern Lake Champlain. They then rowed northward on Champlain, by-passing Ticonderoga and fortified Crown Point, to pursue raids in the middle of French dominated territory.

The whaleboats were used to return to southern Champlain, then were abandoned as the Rangers took to foot travel up and over the mountain ridge to their home base. The craft were found shortly after. The French reported the discovery of four, one of them mounted with swivel guns. Other equipment included a barrel of powder, some balls and grenades and about 40 oars. Said de Bougainville in the Fall of 1756, commenting on the startling discovery:

"It is still to be learned by what route these 'barges' got to Lake Champlain."

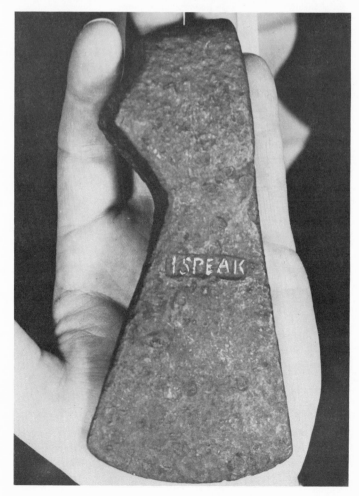

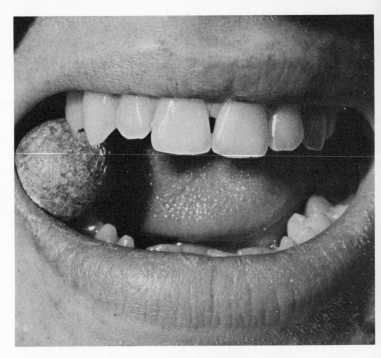

Left: Early "pain killer." Victims of French and Indian War injuries were often given not only heavy doses of rum but musket balls to gnash during the agony of surgery. At left is a leaden ball heavily chewed by a victim of such an operation. At right: Illustration how the ball was held before the operation was performed. Both found on Rogers Island.

He could not envision transportation of the boats up and over trailless mountains. Had he known he would have been properly astonished. But, then, Rogers and his men accomplished many remarkable tasks. It was not uncommon for Rangers to scout Fort Ticonderoga from within musket shot range. They captured prisoners within sight of fort defenders. They harassed convoys in all seasons, fading from sight into the shadows of the forest. They often watched French labor battalions building Fort Ticonderoga from the top of what is known today as Mt. Defiance, a privately owned mountain whose peak is accessible by road. James Lonergan is president of the group which operates it.

These were the days of glory for Rogers and his men, the formative years, the years filled with the excitement of the creation of a fighting force never to be ignored by history. The Rangers fought in other bloody British arenas but there can be no denial they were born as a unit in the Adirondack region and there, in the mountains, tempered into steel. And from among their ranks there arose such leaders as John Stark and Israel Putnam, men who in years to come would attain leadership in the American Revolution.

Rogers himself, when the Revolution approached, was torn between both sides. He chose the British crown. One might charitably say he hoped thereby to gain monies he felt owed to him for past services. During the Revolution he created the Queen's Ranger's but they never matched the muscular, reckless crew of buccaneers he headed in earlier years. It is thought by some he may have figured in the capture of Nathan Hale but the point is debatable. At any rate, he was suspect

to Washington and other American leaders. And his drinking had mounted into a major problem.

One can sit back and wonder what this remarkable man, who fought and lived as best he knew how, thought as his last days approached in the dingy, single room in which he lived at Southwark, England.

Were his drunken ravings flashbacks to the Battle on Snowshoes? Did they include that period of life when he was married, and then divorced? Did they include memories of his remarkable expedition in 1759 to the Indian village of St. Francis in Canada, when he and his men destroyed that hive of conspiracy where Indians plotted and from which they began pillaging forays into northeastern frontier states? Did he re-live, as he coughed blood, the assault on Ticonderoga under the inept Gen. Abercrombie?

Nobody will ever know. Rogers' landlord, who heard his shouts as he lay in his final agonies, did not record them for posterity. Perhaps some mortal remains exist of the Rangers on Mt. Pelee. But swirling throughout that area, as in Southwark, there are only memories which cannot be transcribed.

One thing which cannot be denied, however, is that in the Adirondacks Rogers began a career never duplicated. He was a Viking on land, truly a Goliath in Green, and the path he cut was truly extraordinarily wide and dramatic. The shouts, the curses, the howls and cries of agony are long gone from Mt. Pelee. But even today, as boaters and water skiers whip by its base, unconcerned with what happened two centuries ago, the figure of Major Robert Rogers cannot be forgotten in Adirondack history.

Hundreds of skeletons rest in and around the vicinity of Fort William Henry. Some show cause of death. Note the musket ball in the left elbow of this figure, believed to be one of Rogers' men buried at the Fort. Lower photo shows enlargement of area. Because of insufficient medical care, small wounds sometimes became infected, led to certain death during the French and Indian War period.

Above: Earl Stott, whose holdings on Rogers Island at Fort Edward include the area used by the military during the French and Indian War, pictured near remains of the military hospital in which victims of that war were treated. Photo at left shows "rum mug" found on the island. The tedious, sometimes harsh life of regular soldiers and Rogers Rangers had few pleasant moments. The drinking of rum and other intoxicating beverages was one.

One of the more unusual sketches of Major Robert Rogers, this one picturing an Indian chief offering him a wampum belt. Drawing from the Fort Ticonderoga Museum.

Statue of Sir William Johnson in Johnstown, N.Y., site of his Colonial period home.

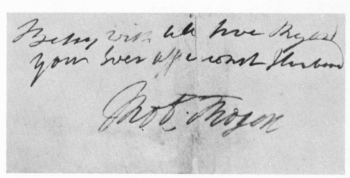

Signature of Major Rogers copied from a letter he sent to his wife. Letter owned by Fort Ticonderoga.

Dr. William H.H. Parkhurst

The Case of the Stone Baby

A year following the death of the widow of Amos Eddy of Herkimer County in 1852, Dr. William H. H. Parkhurst, friend and attending physician during the latter part of her life, stood before the Herkimer County Medical Society, shuffled papers before him, and began:

". . . .I present the following short history of a case which, however uninteresting it may be to the Society, must be considered most certainly as one of a very singular and very rare occurrence."

He thereupon proceeded to describe a case which indeed was very "singular and rare."

Mrs. Eddy, it seems, had been pregnant for 50 years! And at age 77 she had expired, still with the child within her body.

I became aware of the Eddy lithopedion (calcified fetus) when doing a story on a similar child, the famous "stone baby" which figured prominently in the historical novel, "Canal Town," by Samuel Hopkins Adams. In this instance, a physician obtained the specimen at a graveyard autopsy and thus saved his professional reputation. This unborn child is at the Farmers Museum in Cooperstown, partially hidden in the reconstruction of an old-time doctor's office. Why it is not better displayed is a point of wonderment; most certainly it is a provocative display.

While no graveyard scandal is attached to the Eddy child, it is of equal, if not greater interest.

It would not be an understatement to say Mrs. Eddy was an unusual woman. She married in 1795 at age 20 in New Lebanon, Columbia County, shortly afterward moved with her husband to Herkimer County. Amos Eddy died at 70, never to see the startling physical result of his marriage.

Seven years after Mrs. Eddy became a bride, she became pregnant. Her early months produced the usual symptoms. Dr. Parkhurst in his paper said "the catamenial secretion which had always shown itself in a proper manner before this, and which had made its appearance about the age of 14, now ceased, attended more or less with a fulness of blood about the head with nausea and occasionally vomiting, and many other symptoms which usually accompany this important change of system."

As months went by, Mrs. Eddy happily felt life within her. As the eighth month approached, all preparations were made for the birth of the first born. But at eight-and-one-half months, Mrs. Eddy, preparing dinner in a pot suspended from a crane in the family fireplace, received a shock when the crane gave way and contents of the pot spilled into the fire. Two or three hours later labor pains arrived. Birth, it was thought, was imminent. Mrs. Eddy was ordered to bed.

By morning the pains disappeared. Days went by, mounting into anxious weeks. Mr. Eddy kept his horse and buggy in readiness for three weeks, but as time went on, the horse was put to pasture and the buggy went into the barn. More weeks passed. Mrs. Eddy's health began to fail. Doctors were called from the entire area.

"Though all thought that it was some peculiar growth of the Uterus," said Dr. Parkhurst in his report, "none could believe it to be a child. Month after month rolled away and at the expiration of about one year and one half, her health began slowly to improve; though the bulk of abdomen, which had been very large, did not diminish but little, perhaps no more than by absorption of the adipose matter which was deposited in the abdominal cavity."

Eventually full health and vigor returned to Mrs. Eddy, but physical manifestations of pregnancy never left. Thirty years after her first signs, she was still undergoing periodic moments of labor. On one occasion a physician, a Dr. Budlong, arrived at her home after considerable difficulty in travel, examined her, found "nothing abnormal in any of the parts." But Mrs. Eddy said had he been present when she first sent for him "she knew he would have delivered her of her burden." In which case, of course, it would have been a 30-year old newborn!

Photo of the famous lithopedian, or "stone baby" which was carried by a Herkimer County woman for a half century. Calcified fetus is now in the possession of the Albany Medical College.

Dr. Parkhurst became acquainted with the unfortunate woman in 1842, 40 years after first signs of pregnancy. He attended her from then to her death in 1852. Following her demise, a post mortem was conducted in the presence of about 20 persons, described as "mostly aged matrons."

A Utica paper, reporting the scene, said:

"To the utter astonishment of all present, a full grown child was found, encased in a sort of bony or cartilagenous structure, except one leg and foot, and one elbow, which were almost entirely ossified."

The baby was six pounds in weight; before extraction its face and front "looking towards the spine of the mother." Commented Dr. Parkhurst in his report to the medical society: "It had no adhesions or connections with the mother except to the Falopian Tubes and the blood vessels which nourished it, and which were given off from the mesenteric arteries."

Oddly enough the sex of the child was not mentioned. Nor was it specified in a letter to Dr. Parkhurst from Dr. Alden March, founder of Albany Medical College and later of the New York State Medical Society, in which Dr. Alden acknowledged the contribution of the lithopedion to the college museum.

Dr. Parkhurst was born in Herkimer County in 1813. He was graduated from Fairfield Medical College with honors in 1839 and practiced in Herkimer County until his death in 1901. He was elected to the Herkimer County Medical Society in 1840 and to the state group in 1863. His granddaughter, Mrs. Grace Parkhurst Bernard, a one time employe of the New York State Health Department, saw the lithopedion in 1899, again several years later. She was told it was used in the study of anatomy and pathology.

Whatever its use, it remains an extraordinary example of medical history in a western Adirondack county, unbelievable to some, but a fact of life nevertheless.

Charles R. Severance

Diary of a Man Hunt

Assistant District Forest Ranger Charles R. Severance of North Creek, President of Forest Ranger Local 1872, took part in the dramatic sweep for murder suspect Robert Garrow Sr. during 1973. This is his account of the search, which involved hundreds of Forest Rangers, Conservation Officers and State Police.

"A traumatic experience for all, a profoundly moving series of events for me. I have wracked my brain to think of some manner of writing this story to convey at least a hint of the atmosphere that pervasively swirled and eddied through every hamlet, campsite, parking area, up every trail, down every stream, across the ponds and faded away into the Adirondack spruce and balsam; to paint a word picture of the horror, the incredulous disbelief in crimes the nature of which were so alien to this area."

Severance's diary starts July 19, with the report of a "lost couple," Donald Porter and Susan Petz, in the Waddell Road section, in the triangle between the Hudson and Rtes. 8-28. At first it was thought the couple had joined Boston students on a survival course, part of which involved rubber-rafting the Upper Hudson. A raft was found in the abandoned car of the couple. However, shortly after a search was instituted, the body of Porter was found, stabbed three times.

(The badly decomposed body of Miss Petz was found with stab wounds Dec. 1, in an abandoned iron mine shaft at Mineville, Essex County, less than a mile from the childhood home of Garrow Sr.)

While the Porter-Petz search went on, Forest Rangers continued other chores; one was locating children lost in the Blue Mt. Lake Region; they were found by Jim White and John Dalton. The Porter-Petz search was merely a prelude to a far grimmer and more dangerous one.

During it, Rangers helped State Police investigate the "confession" of an area man — proved false — that he had killed Susan Petz and buried her body in a beaver flow, an area flooded by beaver dams. During that same search, Rangers uncovered poaching activities, a salt lick alongside a flow.

During this time, Severance found he had become a grandfather; "I am probably the only man in history to have become a grandfather while standing chest deep in swamp water!" This was July 29, after his daughter, Cathy, 22, married to Wayne Kimmerley of North Troy, gave birth at Glens Falls Hospital. Severance cannot forget that date for two reasons. One is the birth of his grandson. The other is that while he and fellow Rangers were wringing out their clothes from the immersion in the beaver flow, they got word from SP Inspector Henry McCabe to "proceed with all haste" to Gilmantown Road, near Speculator, miles distant.

Events had taken a far worse turn: Murder had been added to murder. Philip Domblewski, 18, of Schenectady, camping with three companions, had been found tied to a tree, stabbed in the chest several times. His companions, also tied, had managed to escape. Now the diary turns to Monday, July 30, 5:30 a.m., as Severance appeared on the Gilmantown Rd. scene:

"**WAS AMAZED** to see group after group of troopers, armed with shotguns, semi-automatic carbines and bolt action rifles. Ran into Marty Hanna immediately, armed with a short single-barrel, leading a group into near-zero-visibility woods. The murder suspect had run a road

Trooper M.J. Masterpolo keeps lonely vigil on bridge over the Sacandaga River during Garrow search. He was one of hundreds of State Police, Forest Rangers and Conservation Officers participating in the dramatic sweep of the wilderness.

block below Fly Creek at 1:30 a.m., had deserted his car at the old mill site on Robbs Creek after a high speed chase. He had fled into the woods up Robbs Creek and the bloodhounds were in there trying to ferret him out. Ninety troopers were in the area, along with BCI and deputies on road blocks. Marty Hanna, Ed Reid, Frank Wagoner, Don Perryman, Dave Larabee and myself from the department.

"On the way down Rte. 8 I noted four Massachusetts cars, one Vermonter and one New Yorker parked at the entrance to the Siamese Pond trail. I found Inspector McCabe and he sent me to Major Walter Stainkamp of SP, and after I explained Siamese Ponds and County Line Creek lay right in the path of a man fleeing farther northward, with the attendant possibility of taking of hostages, he detailed three troopers for me to start to Siamese.

"**NO SIGN** of the fugitive at some closed camps on the west bank of the Sacandaga River near Griffin. Later in the week he broke into one, got a plastic tarp and some peanut butter. Sometime later a positive identification of the suspect was made.

"All camps in the area, at least 40, being methodically searched. At home, the phone rang constantly, either with inquiries about Cathy or about progress of the search. Every half hour, news bulletins, each one a

bit more grim. Tude (Patricia, Severance's wife) says town has rocked with rumors all day. Took a long time to get to sleep, trying to figure where Garrow might be heading. To Siamese? To Rte. 8 out to County Line or Rte. 28 via Big Brook at Indian Lake? He sure has a hell of a lot of choices. Surely he'll try to get some wheels under him. Got to hit a road somewhere to steal a car."

ON THE FOLLOWING day, July 31, Severance mentioned SP helicopters flying over the area, broadcasting messages from Garrow's wife and son. "Garrow was not impressed. Search of camps still going on, also line searches of 20-30 men lined abreast, busting brush in different areas. Not a trace. Bloodhounds were caged, waiting for a fresh opportunity to get on his track, handlers getting impatient to get going on the job.

"At dusk the varied parties started straggling in, sweatsoaked, wet to the knees, tired and hungry. Also angry. Some damned fool who put up lunches must have thought the men were all on a diet, supplied a dab of mayonnaise between two slices of bread for each man's fare.

"There were about 150 troopers in the scene today, bulging the accommodations in Wells and Speculator. Many tourists packed up and left; roadblocks were busy checking out trunks of out-bound traffic. No sight-seers allowed in search areas.

"I GOT HOME after dark, found the house in a virtual state of siege. The kitchen table was piled with guns, ammunition, cleaning rods and old rags and Scott (Severance's 14-year old son) was diligently getting field mice nests out of pieces that hadn't been fired in years.

"My wife had dug out her .44 Special Peacemaker and was busy thumbing in a cylinder full of handloads, at the same time explaining a rumor had hit North Creek that Garrow had positively been seen just below Bakers Mills. Rumors also had him at Indian Lake and also at the A & P parking lot in Warrensburg.

"AGAIN THE phone had rung itself almost off the desk, mostly from women on the verge of hysteria. The news was again grim, as new items of Garrow's record were made public. Lady and Krista, our watch dog Labradors, were snoring unconcernedly at the foot of various beds. I had a hell of a time getting the deadlock on the back door snapped, as it had never been operated in the 25 years we have lived here, and when I got into bed shortly after midnight, I banged my knuckles on the .44 laying next to the ashtray on the night stand.

"Took a long time to get to sleep, wondering what strategy was going to be employed to get Garrow into the open. Maybe the waiting game, seal off all known exits from the area, hoping he makes the attempt? Conduct a massive 'still drive' toward an equally massive 'watch-line?' Send out 'pussyfoot patrols.' World War Two South Pacific style? Tough decisions facing someone."

(SEVERANCE IS A Marine veteran of the South Pacific campaign in the second World War. About his wife's gun: She is an excellent markswoman; won the .44 special in a contest.)

On Aug. 1, the search continued amidst growing rumors of every kind. Marty Hanna, leading a party near Owl Pond, broke radio silence with the report a red shirt had been found just off trail. On Aug. 2, Garrow was still loose and area terror continued to mount; he was spotted near Georgia Brook near the Warren Hamilton County line. He was wearing a blue shirt, replacing the red one.

It was on Aug. 3 searchers found the lean-to Garrow made near a parking area on Rt. 8. Here he waited for some motorist to park. Here was found a live round of 30-30 ammunition. The lean-to, says Severance, was "well camouflaged. Bloodhounds followed his scent about a mile into Georgia Brook territory, then lost it."

RUMORS OF WILD varieties continued, says Severance; one involved a report by a Warrensburg woman that a man fitting Garrow's description went by her home on a bicycle. Police chased the cyclist, found him to be a "highly upset employe of the Warrensburg bank".

"When I arrived home," said Severance, "I found Cathy back from the hospital and with the new baby asleep in its crib, she was out in the meadow banging away at an empty can with the 9 mm Luger. Wayne was loading clips for her and getting in a shot or two with the Smith and Wesson .22. At this moment it sounds both comical and incongruous, but at the time it did not.

"All over the Adirondacks loaded guns were leaned up against doorframes or in bedroom corners, ammunition and padlocks were disappearing from dealers' shelves, and people were discovering the sort of fear that once was the sole province of the inner cities."

THAT SAME day Bill Houck, Mike Hagadorn, Dave Ames and Howard Lashway, armed, prepared to stay in the woods for two or three days. "Once more," says Severance, "sleep came on leaden feet and at 3 a.m., I was in the kitchen checking gear and making a pot of coffee."

On Aug. 5, Adirondack temperatures dropped to 40 degrees; without a cloud cover, there could have been frost. Rangers and troopers met in a conference and it was then that a pattern of movement on Garrow's part evolved, pieced together by two sightings, locations of

A State Trooper checks his bolt action rifle during a period of the long search.

Member of the State Police looks over the overnight shelter of small trees and branches used by alleged killer Robert Garrow, Sr., near a parking area in the Speculator region.

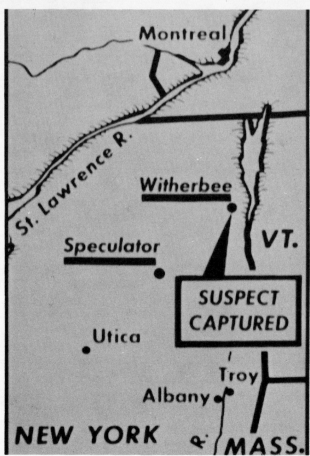

several of his brush wickiups. Total radio silence was being observed, except that search teams were to report every four hours. Road-blocks were expanded. It was at this time State Police related some facts that the news media had not learned.

State Police, says Severance, "reiterated Garrow was extremely dangerous but it was very important he be brought in alive, if possible. The BCI would be sent in to do any shooting if Garrow were cornered and did not give up willingly." The Rangers were told to fire only if their lives were endangered.

THE MEETING preceeded another probe into the woods; stations were set up, one of them on a small rise where the Sacandaga River could be watched, as well as a dim trail Garrow was known to have used. The day ended with nothing positive. Said Severance:

"Everybody seems to be feeling a letdown, with no activity from Garrow for three days. Does it mean he managed to get out of the area, or is he hidden, waiting for a break? Will he be traveling tonight or early in the morning? What's going to happen if he tangles with one of the teams?"

Severance left the scene for home at 8 p.m., found a note on the kitchen table from his 20 year-old daughter, Jan, asking for a gun and shells which she wished to carry in the car on a trip the following day. "She's edgy," writes Severance, "and I can't blame her; nine miles of uninhabited woods roads at 5 o'clock in the morning."

"DOWNTOWN AFTER cigarettes," reads Severance's diary. "I think a Conservation Officer would have a field day; about half the cars I see have rifles or shotguns in the seats and I'll bet all of them are loaded. Rumors flying in every direction; Garrow has been seen everywhere but in Skylab. People are reacting. Tude told me Blanch Alexander, North Creek, sat up all last night in a chair by the front door, with a pair of fireplace tongs across her knees.

"Back home I went to sleep. At 3 a.m., I was bolt upright, dripping with cold sweat from a nightmare... Garrow had forced Jan's car into the abutment of Boreas bridge and her screams were ringing in my ears. No more sleep. Down to the kitchen in the weak moonlight to make a pot of coffee, wondering if Garrow were using that same source of illumination to find an opening he can slip through."

ON AUG. 6, three days before Garrow was cornered and shot, Severance, up at 5 a.m., said the thermometer dropped to 40 again. "I felt a chill, too," he says, "but not entirely from the morning air as I half expected to hear a flurry of shots somewhere back in the woods as Garrow made one of his usual early morning tours."

No activity except usual ones at roadblocks; troopers reported not too much traffic. But rumors continued; Garrow seen at Inlet, Indian Lake. One this day the feeling was becoming evident Garrow was out of the Speculator area, with transportation, but still armed. Said Severance: "We're still all wound up like a spring after another day of inaction."

Aug. 7 came with its dramatic aspects. Garrow had run a second roadblock, had escaped State Police in the Indian Lake area after the SP car engine "blew up." Then came reports of the Garrow sighting at a North Creek gas station; then came reports of his presence in Witherbee. The search thereupon contracted in the area, the noose, everyone felt, was tightening. And indeed it was. The following day Rangers were also faced with investigating a suicide atop Pok-O-Moonshine Mountain, a hanging. Severance also made note of a memo from the Department of Environmental Conservation saying Rangers and Conservation Officers were acting on their own at roadblocks and in the woods.

Every day during the search for Garrow the routine was the same. Here a Forest Ranger drives a vehicle of armed men to an area where once again the hunt fanned out.

Relentlessly the hunt for Garrow went on, day and night. Above, Troopers inspect cars on road leading to Speculator. At left WRGB newsman Jim Williams goes "topless" in the heat of the day as he writes copy for his newscast. He was one of scores of newsmen assigned to the man hunt.

"IF THE MEMO was actually a statement of policy," wrote Severance, "could it be interpreted to say a Ranger on a roadblock or in the woods with the SP was on his own literally, with no protection from civil liability that might arise through his actions?" He continued: "No sightings of Garrow in the Witherbee area today. SP getting an unwarranted sandbagging from some sources. Very few seem to realize the odds have been with Garrow right along."

Aug. 9 entry: "The manhunt is over! Sometime about 2:30 p.m. Garrow was flushed by bloodhounds out of thicket at Witherbee, driven to a watchline of men cordoning off the area, and gunned down by one of four shotgun blasts from a Conservation Officer. Seriously wounded, but going to live. Now if they can get him to tell where the Petz girl can be found."

Thus the end of the Diary of a Manhunt. The finale saw Garrow cornered; four Rangers, Case Phinney, Dick Olcott, Bruce Coon and John Maye heard him moving through the brush. Hillary LeBlanc, Conservation Officer, saw him, fired. Garrow moved a short distance and was captured. The hunt was over.

Garrow subsequently was charged with the murder of young Domblewski, and following hospital treatment in Plattsburgh was lodged in the Hamilton County jail. As of this writing he had not been charged with the other homicides.

Roadside scene, top photo, taken at spot where Garrow was cornered and shot by a conservation officer, thus ending the long search. Lower photo: A typical scene on roads both in the Speculator and Mineville sections. Trooper checks cars passing through his assigned area.

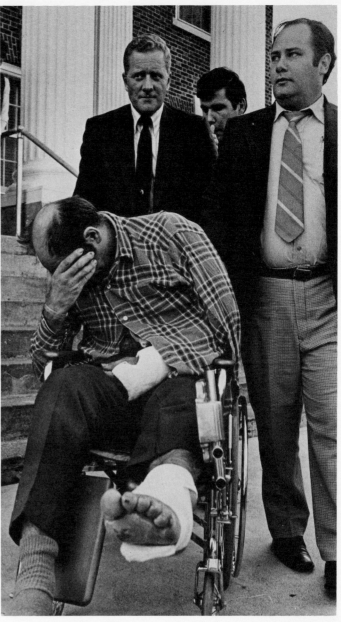

Top: Robert Garrow, Sr., suspected killer, and object of a wilderness search. At right: After treatment at a Plattsburgh Hospital, Garrow, in wheelchair, was removed to the Hamilton County Jail at Lake Pleasant. News photos used through courtesy of Capital Newspapers; photographers included Fred McKinney, Paul D. Kniskern, Bob Paley and Jack Madigan.

So Proudly We Sailed

Lake Champlain Is Famous For Many Things,
But Mostly As The Birthplace Of The World's Second
Successful Steamship; The First American Navy, And
The Last Of The Sidewheelers, The Ticonderoga.

Reproduction of watercolor of Battle of Valcour Island by a British Officer, H. Gilder. Painting on display at Smithsonian Institution, Washington, D.C., as part of Philadelphia exhibit.

The lake "discovered" by the French explorer Samuel de Champlain after native born Americans had paddled its waters for thousands of years, sprawls and flows about 110 miles south to north from Whitehall, N. Y., to Missisquoi Bay, Canada.

It covers almost 500 square miles and in its deepest spot, north of Westport, you'd need 400 feet of line to hook a bottom feeding fish. Its width is about 12 miles between Burlington, Vt. and the New York shore and it is of such generous proportions researchers estimate it takes a full century to flush itself; that is, water in the basin today will be replaced 100 years hence by new supplies.

(Lake George, by comparison, which flows into Champlain, takes an estimated ten years for a full flush).

Lake Champlain thus is deep enough, wide enough, long enough to foster legends. One is, of course, of a supposed monster lurking in its depths, a sort of miniature Loch Ness beast, described as "black and serpentine." To date it has been reported seen by boaters as recently as in the Spring of 1973, and others have literally reported riding the swells created by its undulating movements. If anyone has tried capture, the effort has not succeeded. If the story is true, the muscular monster has mastered longevity and may replenish itself at some Fountain of Youth disgorging precious waters in some underwater cavern.

At the same time the huge lake has furnished other forms of drama since the day Champlain shot up a bunch of aggressive Iroquois on Ticonderoga's shoreline in 1609.

Drama on this inland sea does not die easily. Nor will it ever in the case of three unusual, wide bottomed ladies who gallantly plowed their way through the waves and moods of the lake, lived their allotted spans, and in due course ended remarkable careers in startlingly different fashions.

One torpedoed herself with her own connecting rod in the Richelieu River through which Champlain funnels itself into the St. Lawrence River.

That was the Vermont, launched at Burlington in 1808, shortly after Robert Fulton sailed his Clermont on Hudson's River. Fulton's craft is considered the first successfully operated commercial steamboat in the world. The Vermont is considered the second, despite certain peculiarities of maneuver epitomized in the name affectionately given by passengers, the "old sawmill."

She floated and sounded like one. On occasion, the story goes, her gasps, grunts and groans aroused glandular response in many a romantic bull moose diving for water plants along the lake's shore line. The Vermont was the first sidewheeler to ply with what one might term "regularity with qualifications" on any lake in the world.

The second ship entered her tomb with grace and dignity. She descended evenly, gently and with decorum into the murky depths for good and sufficient reason. A 24-pound solid ball of iron, fired from a British cannon in October, 1776, performed an unexpected tracheotomy on her starboard side, just below the water line, and that wound settled her into her grave as gently as an

Autumn leaf falls upon placid waters. Not even shoes hastily kicked off by crew members diving frantically overboard were disturbed; no iron kettle in her open cooking fireplace was jarred; not even her glass sand clock was knocked askew.

Champlain's waters received her with a mother's embrace; closed upon her with the firmness and inexorability of a Venus fly trap, but never did quite get around to total digestion.

That ship was the Revolutionary War gunboat, the Philadelphia, sawed from virgin timber, hammered and forged into creation at Whitehall as one of the miserably equipped units in America's first Naval fleet.

The third ship came to no violent end, nor did it come to a sad one. No northern pike was destined to swim leisurely through submerged staterooms or lounges, eating smelt fry off the captain's table. On the contrary, in one of the most spectacular cross-country moves of the century, this vessel was transported overland on rails laid on frozen ground, from her Champlain water bed to a permanent dry dock on land at the Shelburne Museum at Shelburne, Vt. That ship, of course, was the 892-ton Ticonderoga, built in 1906. She was the last of the sidewheelers on Lake Champlain. The twilight of steam became night when finally she settled in her dry land cradle.

I became well acquainted with all three over a period of years as a feature writer for The Times-Union. All left memories.

The Vermont, sad to say, is no more; during the 1950's what was salvaged of her punctured and fire-seared carcass was transported by flat bed truck to an area on the Port Kent Road, near Ausable Chasm, ostensibly to become an exhibit in an American Naval Museum which unfortunately never materialized. Today much of the ship has returned to the soil; some ribs and boards, however, remain in a barn at Willsboro Point.

My first encounter with what was left of the old saw-mill came in 1954 shortly after it was raised from the Richelieu, floated southward and beached on the New York shore.

I recall the incident clearly. It was a dismal, rainy night, shrouded with fog, when Fred Fraser, a friend from the Schenectady Gazette and I reached the old hull. My first impression, registered as headlights of my car created scores of grotesque shadows, was literally that a gaunt dinosaur of a departed age had risen in agony from the dark waters, gasping for breath, and had flung its naked and glistening bones upon the beach.

Most assuredly it was not the Vermont as once the craft existed. Not even nearly so. Only the bottom half of the hull of stout oak ribs and boards held together. Its engine and all other moving metal parts had been removed shortly after its connecting rod did its own early 19th century version of acupuncture, some six years after the boat's commission.

These, I learned, were placed on another boat on Champlain. That craft also had a short life because in 1817 the James Caldwell, first steamboat on Lake George, was launched, and the original Vermont engine, a 20-horsepower job with a cylinder of 20 inches and a three foot piston stroke powered that vessel.

(Interesting to note here is that owners of the James Caldwell were not the luckiest of ship owners. While chimney swifts did not nest in her innovative brick smokestack, lightning did briefly. And the boat much later burned at her Lake George dock. Arson, encouraged by what some called "over insurance" was suspected, never proved. Where the historic engine is today, I do not know. It could be buried deep in the mud bottom of Lake George. Or, for that matter, it might be a conversation piece in the cellar den of some New Jersey skin diver, of the type who has plucked historic wonders from Lake George over the years and conveniently forgotten to notify New York State authorities of such recoveries).

The Vermont lasted only six years which figure by coincidence matches her top speed limit. She never, obviously, quite recovered from the hangover created by the jug of potent Vermont rum smashed across her bow during launching. Later sailing proved it. She was steered by a tillerman who on demand (which was often) was assisted by deckhands rolling barrels from one side to another to shift weight to assist the craft in changing course. On occasion passengers shifted positions for the same purpose. So did horses, when they were carried.

The Vermont was eight feet deep, had a 20-foot beam and was 167 tons burden. In keeping with the frequent, understandable moods of her harassed captain she was painted black. Her construction cost was an estimated $20,000 and launching was not without ponderable, dire implication to sailors of the lake; half way down the skids she got stuck.

Sometimes it took her a week to make the lake circuit, provided her boiler developed no leaks and, in event it did, her engineer had enough lead on hand to plug them. Passengers generally boarded by catching up with rowboats. When she did manage to stop to discharge freight or clients, the latter were usually given two hour warnings of the impending miracle.

The Vermont's sanitation facilities were unusual in that their use was at times in direct conflict with Nature's time table; gentlemen, for instance, were allowed to use the washrooms in the order in which they paid their fares. To the man with abdominal pressures, such a procedure often caused consternation.

Ladies were given far better courtesies; this was, one must remember, long before Women's Lib and assertions of equal privileges came into being. There were other rules aboard this historic tub rigidly enforced. One was that no male passenger was allowed to sleep with his boots on. Another prohibited the singing of such lusty songs as "Burgoyne's Defeat," or "Clinton's March." The Revolution in the early 1800's was still memory; Captain John Winans had no desire for reenactment of the late Rebellion aboard his ship.

In the War of 1812, when England for some unfathomable reason desired the return of American colonies, the Vermont transported troops and horses; once was almost captured by the British but a Vermont smuggler overheard the plan, warned Captain Winans and was paid a whopping $10 for his information. The smuggler caught up with the Vermont the usual way, by rowboat.

When this unusual craft sunk in the Richelieu, she settled in about 15 feet. Divers in 1954, prowling the hull, were handicapped in fondling her remains by a considerable number of broken bottles on board. This, in turn, led to the story that all was not quite the picture of sobriety when the ship scuttled herself.

Supervisor Edward Hatch of Willsboro Point, a real estate and insurance man, son of the late Payson E. Hatch, one of those involved in the 1954 salvage, told me research by the late Lorenzo Hagglund, another interested salvager, revealed the existence of a party on the ship and from the number of smashed bottles, it must have been a swinger. Consumption of alcoholic beverages was not uncommon; as a matter of fact, "fines" levied from violators of ship's rules went into a common fund from which "wine for the company" was purchased. In this way many were able not only to toast their shipboard sins but enjoy them.

Payson Hatch, a friend of mine, served as president of the organization salvaging the Vermont. Hagglund, an experienced deep sea diver, was vice-president and John

F. Kiehl, a perfume expert of national repute, served as treasurer in this informal group.

Raising of the Vermont was accomplished with oil drums. In Supervisor Hatch's barn today remain some ribs and boards. The rest of the old hulk is long gone. What was to be its final resting place is now a privately owned, public campground. During the Fall of 1973 I walked the grounds for more than an hour, found no mound of rotting timbers, no trace of where the hull had been deposited. Reconstructing the ship would have cost a fortune, even in 1954. There just wasn't enough of the old craft left and no detailed plans exist of her original construction.

Apparently she was built as she sailed — by whim.

The staunch Philadelphia is another story entirely. Today this priceless relic of the Revolutionary War fleet built under the verbal whiplash of Benedict Arnold rests in the Smithsonian Institution in Washington, D. C. Her 59-foot length and 15-foot beam; her planked hull are all suitably and excellently displayed. Thus more lost treasure insofar as New York State is concerned, never to grace the new museum in the billion dollar South Mall in Albany, never to return to the state in which the ship was born.

In 1965 I talked with Dr. Philip K. Lundeberg, curator of Naval History at the Smithsonian. He told me only one other exhibit in the Philly's area outranked the ship in interest and that was the original Star Spangled Banner.

The Vermont, world's second successful steamship, is long gone, but this wooden model gives some idea of what the "old sawmill" looked like in her days of glory on Lake Champlain.

The "old sawmill," as the Vermont, world's second successful steamboat was called, is pictured in this painting, used by courtesy of the National Life Insurance Company. The ship, while a sensation, had several peculiar habits of maneuver; eventually sank in the Richelieu River, through which Lake Champlain flows into the St. Lawrence.

Top left: Lorenzo Hagglund inspects rib of Vermont. Top right: The remains of the ship on Champlain's shores. Lower left: Payson Hatch points to metal casing where the paddle wheel axle once rested. Other photo: One of the military buttons found when Vermont's remains were salvaged.

The Philadelphia, like other vessels in the American fleet, was born of desperation. A British squadron planned to move southward on Lake Champlain as part of a master plan to split the colonies. The Americans had nothing to stop it. Typically American, they thereupon pulled out their own do-it-yourself kits of the day and built their own fleet from raw lumber in the Whitehall area. Without the aggressive Arnold it is doubtful if the ships would have materialized. Congress held off until early 1776 to order him to prepare for the British assault. By October his fleet included eight gundelos (gunboats), four row galleys and a few others. As usual, during the Revolution, it was the American chihuahua pitted against the English mastiff.

Arnold had other problems. American archives reveal at least 5,000 qualified seamen serving in the Continental Army. But Arnold had only 70 with him when after one short shakedown cruise he took to the open lake to meet the British in the Battle of Valcour Island. Only a few experienced hands were aboard the Philly; the rest of the crew reflected the usual fighting men of the period, farmers, tinsmiths, carpenters, trappers, coopers, iron workers, tradesmen and the like.

The British outgunned and outmanned the patriots. In the October battle the Philadelphia was promptly punctured by British iron. The ball which sunk her is still embedded, still draws astonishment at the Smithsonian. In succeeding hours vessels in the American fleet were scattered, sunk, burned and some were beached, crews fleeing into surrounding forests, preferring tomahawks of prowling Mohawks to British cannon.

Technically one can say the Americans were defeated. But this is open to argument. The British advance was stopped. The lion had to lick its wounds and took too long a time to do it. A historian, Admiral A. T. Mahan, who much later made an exhaustive study of the battle, wrote:

"That the Americans were strong enough to impose capitulation of Saratoga was due to the invaluable year secured to them in 1776 by their little Navy on Lake Champlain, created by the indomitable courage of the traitor Benedict Arnold."

That much is history. The point today is the Philadelphia is the only complete vessel which survived the holocaust in entirety. And it was found intact by Lorenzo Hagglund, hithertofore mentioned as one of the salvagers of the Vermont.

After the Vermont's skeleton was raised and floated to Champlain's shores, it was hoisted aboard an improvised trailer and hauled to an area on the Port Kent Road, contemplated site of an American Naval Museum which never materialized. This scene depicts one of the stops made during the haulage of the old ship.

Hagglund was an interesting, somewhat puzzling man. He was an experienced prowler of Lake Champlain's gloomy bottom long before modern day skin divers took up the practice in far more efficient equipment. His was the hard hat type of gear. He told me he discovered the ship after studies of the battle led him to an approximate location between Valcour Island and the New York mainland.

He first removed the cannon, then raised the ship, eventually placing it on display in a barge shed near Willsboro. There it remained for many years, visible but not touchable to the public — at 50 cents a visit. A small sign on the highway leading to the shed was its major advertisement. It read: "Revolutionary War Gunboat."

I visited Hagglund often while the ship was on display. He was a man of unusual temperament, taciturn at times, talkative only when he got to know his interviewer. He considered the Philly and all articles on it priceless. As indeed they were to him. How does one set an adequate price upon merchandise hauled from a submerged Pandora's Box of America's past? Eventually, however, a price was settled upon; following Hagglund's death the Smithsonian reportedly paid $25,000 and transportation costs. One can imagine the cost of such an antique today, a decade later.

There was drama in finding the Philadelphia in about 60 feet of water. Hagglund told me that as he walked the bottom of the lake he noted what first appeared to be a "mass of rock" in the translucent distance. But as he continued his slow advance the "rock" became one of definite outline and the outline most assuredly was not shapeless stone.

Hagglund found himself walking into history. The mass was the Philadelphia, resting upright, in all respects in the same position she had descended to the bottom. He circled the vessel, savoring the moment, his pulse admittedly faster, hardly believing his eyes as he viewed the outlines of this astonishing ghost. As he moved, schools of fish darted from its recesses; one flashed from the mouth of a cannon. Hagglund placed his hand on the ship's oak sides. The wood was cold, hard, slippery to the touch.

He boarded, and once aboard, swung his helmet from side to side, taking in treasure undisturbed for 159 years. As he walked, he stirred clouds of cinders; in some areas, they were inches deep. Not until weeks later did he figure out why they had collected. The Philadelphia's grave rested under regular, later steamboat routes and over many years cinders, spewed from funnels, settled and shrouded the gunboat. No passenger of that later day realized what lay immobilized 60 feet below.

Hagglund's visit was literally one to a tomb. Skeletal remains were found; one shoe still contained the bones of a foot, blown off by a cannon ball. Human teeth were found. Hagglund located the sand clock standing upright; the sand flowed freely after the instrument was brought to the surface. It was kept in his private office behind the exhibition shed.

Hundreds of Colonial period relics were scattered about the open vessel, from belt to shoe buckles, from musket to cannon balls. Blackened kettles were still in place in the open pit fireplace. Firewood was still intact, stored under the small foredeck.

The cannon bonanza was impressive. The 12-pounder on the bow ran 3,400 pounds. The two nine pounders which jutted over gunwales on each side ran 1,500 pounds each. They are of Swedish manufacture, were probably "borrowed" from Fort Ticonderoga's arsenal by the impetuous, demanding Arnold. The craft's descent into more than a century-and-one-half of liquid oblivion was so gentle cannon balls, neatly stacked, were not disturbed. Charred embers of wood in the brick fireplace were still in place. Some degree of water wear of the wooden hull was evident, but it was minor.

When Hagglund hauled her out of the lake, the Philadelphia began to dry and peel. No visitor was allowed to touch her; the average tourist, being what he is, would have eliminated the Philly splinter by splinter. Hagglund was on hand to watch every move. For years this utterly irreplaceable relic of America's early muscle rested in a shed whose roof was supported against heavy Winter snows by two-by-fours. The shed was also a fire trap.

When Hagglund died, the Smithsonian was far more alert than New York State. It made an offer to the survivor and it was accepted. The Philly was crated and transported to Washington. Care used was comparable to that tendered a newborn. In a way, of course, the Philadelphia was just that.

In Washington the peeling wood was sprayed with polyethylene glycol and its surface coated with liquid nylon to stop disintegration. Today the vessel is mounted before colored maps and sketches of the battle, one of them by a British officer, H. Gilder. The original is in Windsor Castle, one of the mementos Britain keeps on hand to remind the nation of opportunities lost.

Originally it was planned the Philadelphia would be displayed with the reconstructed Vermont at the contemplated American Naval Museum on the Port Kent Road. Truly it is unfortunate the museum never came into existence. Only a handful of other naval exhibits would have equalled the Philly in general interest.

One, of course, would have been the reconstructed Vermont. If one allows imagination to run, another would have been a salvaged Monitor. Or Fulton's Clermont, Henry Hudson's Halfmoon or, stretching the point even more to imaginative impossibility, Columbus' Santa Maria.

Today America can rest assured the Philadelphia is in good hands. At least it is not a pile of ashes.

Volumes of type have been printed on the Ticonderoga, which went into service in 1906, finished its active career in 1953. My acquaintance with this distinguished member of the sidewheeler clan is confined to its astonishing journey from Lake Champlain to the Shelburne Museum. This was truly an event of gargantuan proportions and of interest to the entire country.

A view of the Philadelphia from floor level at the Smithsonian Institution. Left: The old barge shed which once housed this priceless Revolutionary War relic near Willsboro.

Top: Overall photo of the Philly; note rudder at stern at left. Lower photo taken looking down upon the bow; arrow points to British cannon ball which sunk the historic vessel. All photos of the Philadelphia at the Smithsonian are used through courtesy of that institution.

Above: My first pictorial record of the Philadelphia, showing its position in the shed which served as its home for many years.

Left: Remains of the open fire pit, showing kettles and bricks as found when the ship was salvaged.

Closeups of cannon found aboard the Phila-delphia when Hagglund brought her up from Champlain's bottom. Lower photo is of bow cannon; top photo is one of two which gave her shooting power from both sides. Note cannon balls resting in rows.

It was no easy task. The Ti was built by the Champlain Transportation Company at a cost of $170,000. Today she would cost at least four million, and that may be an understatement. It probably is.

Up to the point where the haulage began, the Ti was merely a name to me. I had never paced her decks, heard her steam whistle, watched the operation of her walking beam, nor had I ever watched her ponderous paddles grip the lake. She was a ship which had carried both freight and passengers, including United States Presidents and European royalty. Listed among more exotic cargos was an elephant.

Campaigns to keep the Ti afloat and in operation failed and finally there was no more money and there just wasn't the public interest. This, understand, was back in the 1950's. There was then no resurgence of interest in steam propelled vessels. Steam was a fossil power of the past. The cannibals of the time were the trucks, the railroads, the passenger cars. Today things might be different. Nostalgia has its grip upon the American mind. Perhaps the Ticonderoga would prove a floating gold mine. Perhaps tourists would flock to it to prove to gaping offspring that indeed steam could do more than make a kettle whistle.

But the Ti was a dead horse in the early 1950's. And the only interested party was the Shelburne Museum, one of the most remarkable historical complexes in the United States. Facing the museum, however, was the problem of getting the Ti to here (the museum) from 'way over there (Lake Champlain).

Merritt-Chapman and Scott sublet the contract to W. H. Hill Company of Tilton, New Hampshire. Officials pondered and planned. Here was a vessel 9,250 feet from the point where the museum wanted it placed. Here was a ship 220 feet long, with a beam of 57-and-one-half feet, with a depth of 11-and-one-half feet. Here were 892 tons of sheer dead weight; a ship with a steel hull, with a W. and A. Fletcher reciprocating vertical beam; powered by one cylinder of 53 inches bore and a nine foot stroke. The weight of the piston alone was three tons. Two boilers were aboard, fire tube, return flue, 750 horsepower each and hand fired, big enough to consume in fiery fury two tons of coal an hour. The outer shell of the smokestack was six feet in diameter and its height above the hurricane deck was 38 feet.

The enormous paddle wheels were 25 feet in diameter; ten buckets to each wheel, with bucket dimensions 30 inches wide and nine feet long. At full throttle the Ti's power plant drove them 28 full revolutions a minute.

Executive heads were scratched. Out came the idea pads. Down went facts and figures. And heard were groans as the enormity of the project became apparent. Topographical studies of the proposed route were made; grades were analyzed. The first step to haul this historic, inert mass was taken in the Fall of 1954. Lake Champlain never saw anything like what ensued, nor will again unless somebody decides to move the City of Plattsburgh.

The Ticonderoga as she is today at the Shelburne Museum, Shelburne, Vt.

An enormous basin was dredged out of the shoreline. An earthen barrier separated the basin from the lake; the ship had to be raised 16 feet above lake level to position her on railroad flat bed carriers. Once the basin was hollowed out and dirt piled high around it, the barrier between the lake and the man-made basin was opened and Champlain's waters poured in. The Ti was floated into this new bay. The barrier was closed and water from Champlain was pumped into the basin. The task was not easy; leaks were frequent. Essentially what was created was an inland lock. But finally the level rose, the Ti went up with it and was maneuvered over the railroad cradles, lashed into position.

Winter had arrived. In January the monster began its journey, a mechanical King Kong over frozen ground. The first day the ship was moved 150 feet by use of winches on trucks. Sometimes the trucks themselves had to be anchored to trees to withstand the tremendous pull. As fast as rails were used, they were ripped up and positioned ahead. Slowly the work grew more efficient. Eventually the ship was being hauled about 250 feet a day.

Sixty-five days, 20 hours and 28 minutes after she began her journey the Ti was at the museum. Here she was jacked into position and today is visible to startled motorists traveling Route 7.

I visited the Ti often during those days of overland travel and each time marveled at the victory over sudden thaws, sleet storms, snow storms, grades, crossings of highways and even the crossing of a railroad route (one train was held up until the ship "sailed" grandly across its tracks). Each time I could only picture a mouse pulling a dead elephant. But the mouse was Hercules in

disguise, and inches at a time, while men held their breath and prayed, the Ti moved ponderously, slowly, inexorably towards its new home.

Today visitors walk her decks, inspect her engine room, relive bygone days in her luxurious interior. No waves cause gentle heaving of decks; no thunder comes from suppressed steam furious to get at the job of moving the paddle wheels.

Like the Philadelphia, the Ticonderoga, a tangible ghost of the past, now has a permanent home.

Stops were frequent as the Ticonderoga was hauled from Lake Champlain to the Shelburne Museum. Here is one photo, furnished by the Museum, showing the huge sidewheeler as it approached a highway crossing. Plans were so well laid that such crossings were done in minimum time and with little inconvenience.

Lady of the Lake

**Tenaciously She Clung To What
Some Termed Mission Impossible
But Finally Diane Struble
Accomplished Her Dream**

Unrelenting ambition and sheer determination have combined to perfect many an athlete. Some reach the glory heights through long, tedious, tiring hours of practice, each day, each week and month evidence of incredible power of will. Some are born with the perfection of greatness, needing only coaching to loosen the reservoir of energy into winning channels.

The most perfect swimming machine I ever knew was Diane Struble. She was a combination of all factors. She possessed the power and she had the patience to develop it.

That's why she became the first person to swim the length of moody, 32-mile-long Lake George.

Envision a beautifully proportioned body, tireless muscles, total dedication, beauty of movement, consistent faith in the achievement of a set goal.

That was Diane.

I first met this remarkable mermaid, now living in Vermont, when she was 17 years old, a senior at the high school in Scotia, N.Y. At the time I was handling special assignments for the Schenectady Gazette. One day word came through that a girl by the name of Diane Struble was thinking of having a go at Lake George.

That was when I first met her. Her practicing in those days was done in Collins Lake, Scotia. What encouragement I was able to offer I offered. And she did indeed try Lake George.

In August, 1950, she made her first assault, but her courageous attempt failed; a storm whipped up heavy waves during the first part of the eighteen-and-one-half hours she struggled and the storm, in turn, was followed by heavy fog. Accompanying personnel, while capable, numbered too few. At 2:05 a.m., after swimming more than half the distance from Lake George Village to Ticonderoga, her mother, Mrs. Amanda Struble, ordered a reluctant Diane out of the water.

Mrs. Struble estimated her daughter had covered a full 25 miles in a zig-zag course. Diane wanted to continue, but finally consented to give up the attempt. But even as she left the cold waters she had made up her mind that some day, come hell or high water, she was going to complete the course.

That determination never died.

Exercise was the order of the day for Diane as she prepared for her record swim. Here she limbers up before a practice session. Jogging and mountain climbing also were included in her schedule.

Full cooperation for the Struble swim of Lake George was given by the late Sheriff Carl McCoy, one of the most colorful lawmen ever to head Warren County's sheriff's department.

In August, 1951, she entered the Sacandaga Reservoir (now known for some reason or another as the Great Sacandaga Lake) at Northville, fully intending to leave this huge, man-made bathtub at Conklingville, where the dam which gave birth to the reservoir is located. But again weather and logistical support were against her. High winds whipped up rolling waves and after sixteen futile hours she was forced to cease at 2 a.m. Some eighteen miles of the thirty-two mile course had been accounted for. Once she was lost in the darkness. The difficulty here was the same as the first attempt at Lake George. Not only did waves bury her from sight on occasion but supervising personnel again was not sufficient in craft or guiding proficiency.

During intervening years I saw Diane occasionally and Lake George always came into the conversation. Meantime, I had moved on to the Times-Union in Albany. Finally the time did come when the challenge became reality. This time conditions were different. Paul Lukaris, owner of Animal Land, Route 9, just south of Lake George Village, was president of the local Chamber of Commerce. Paul is an enthusiastic man; saw Diane's possibilities and in those possibilities also saw fame for the resort area. He became, in essence, her business manager.

So in 1957 Diane warmed up for her final attack by swimming a round trip between Bolton and Lake George Village. The distance: an estimated 20 miles. She had lost none of her ability; if anything, her endurance had increased. To toughen her leg muscles, she often walked 25 miles a day. Some days she jogged part of the distance. There were times, living in the Schenectady area, when she would walk to the city of Albany and return. This writer, working then as City and Sunday Editor of the Times-Union, often spotted her familiar figure swinging along Route 5. Always she refused offers of rides. Once she did consent to a brief stop. And that was for a cup of coffee.

When in the Lake George area, she thought nothing of climbing 2,000-foot-high Prospect Mountain two or three times a week. Often she jogged rough mountain trails for miles.

Lukaris had interested many others in her contemplated attempt. And this time there was more than enough cooperation, and there was solid planning. There were, for instance, Warren County Sheriff's boats as well as volunteer private craft. Helpers were on hand aplenty. The idea, the challenge, had taken hold.

Also, this time, Diane's advisors suggested tackling the lake from Ticonderoga south to Lake George to take advantage of prevailing winds.

Superbly conditioned, indomitably infused, she coated her body with five pounds of grease to ward off the cold waters and on Friday, August 22, 1958, flat-ironed into the water at Ticonderoga's shore at 10:30 a.m.

Lake George may be the "Queen of Lakes," but the old girl has moods one can hardly describe as royal. For days this huge expanse of cold, spring fed water may rest as peacefully as a babe in a warm crib. But she has a quick temper and within twenty minutes, buffeted by winds, she can turn into white-capped fury. Many a boater has learned that lesson the hard way.

Furthermore, there was the question of the route. The lake runs north and south and while the current is northward, this constituted no problem; impact of the current is negligible. The greatest problem was plotting a course that would be almost direct, and keeping Diane on it. The energy-wasting zig-zags of the past were still fresh, unpleasant memories.

Her estimated swimming course actually ran about 41 miles; a straight line north to south was impossible. When finally her effort began, the event was what one might call a "sleeper." Comparatively little attention had been paid in the general media. Only a few of the faithful were on hand to see Diane plane off. The Times-Union, happy to say, covered the event from start to finish.

But as the swim progressed, public attention began to focus upon the lonely figure, swimming in a manner which at first seemed almost casual. For the first mile-and-one-half Diane used the breast stroke. After that it was the Australian crawl. Her starting weight was 147 pounds; during the swim she slimmed down to 131 pounds. That's weight watching the hard way.

As it became obvious she had a good chance to accomplish what had proved impossible to others, radio and newspapers — those not already on the job — began to awaken. During brief "rest" periods, when she slowed her pace, or trod water, she joked with those aboard accompanying boats. Her every move was covered. Sometimes to her disadvantage, thoughtless pilots approached too closely, dosing her lungs with exhaust fumes. These were bull-horned away. When high waves were whipped up by a south wind near Sabbath Day Point, Diane donned goggles.

Friday night the temperature dropped. There was no rest. Her pace was maintained. At 3 a.m. there was hunger; she called for two hamburgers; her restaurant was the water of the lake, eerily lighted by the beams of boat lights.

By this time the public media had spread the word that a physical miracle was occurring at Lake George. Every mile of Diane's progress was reported. As her goal neared, tension increased. Bets were made. Unperturbed, she plowed steadily ahead, fighting off tensing leg muscles. The day wore on; faded into dusk; Saturday's light became Saturday's darkness. Still she kept up her astonishing outpouring of energy; the long walks, the mountain climbing, the jogging, were paying handsome dividends.

Breakfast before her swim? Hardly! Diane consumed a full course dinner before she entered the waters at Ticonderoga. Two big steaks were only part of her "preparatory" meal!

A mile from victory she was still going strong and if a tidal wave had suddenly appeared it couldn't have stopped her. Crowds began to stream onto the Beach Road in the village. When she came into sight, 10,000 were on hand to greet her with a thunderous ovation. The horns of hundreds of autos, jammed into what parking space was available, depleted batteries with their raucous blares. Lake George had never heard such a roar since French cannons blasted Fort William Henry into collapse two centuries before.

An octopus of grasping hands reached down to help her mount the dock; she protested; wanted to do it herself. Nothing doing. She was literally hauled from the dark waters. The time: 10 p.m. She had been in the water for 35 and-one-half hours!

Rushed to a nearby motel, she was examined immediately by a physician, pronounced in excellent condition. I had left the City desk at The Times-Union after seeing to it that most of the Sunday copy had gone over, and arrived too late to see her dramatic finish. I went over to the motel, was refused admittance until Diane heard my voice. I thereupon became a welcome guest. She was resting on a bed. I went over to shake her hand but was bussed instead. That was energy I hadn't counted upon!

Diane's exploits didn't end there. In July, one year later, she swam another irregular course from Burlington, Vt., to Plattsburgh on the New York side of Champlain, to the cheers of another crowd numbering in the thousands. But this one was understandably irregular in performance and filled with stark danger; Champlain's waves, raised by wind to ugly proportions, often buried her from sight of accompanying boats and often contact was by sound only.

In August, the same year, she visited New York City. And while visiting, astonished the inhabitants of that metropolis by swimming 30 miles around the island of Manhattan, in 11 hours and 27 minutes.

For the girl who conquered Lake George, it was easy.

Top: Personnel assisting Diane in preparation for her swim helped coat her body with five pounds of grease to ward off chilling effects of Lake George's spring fed waters.

Lower photo: Fully ready for the biggest attempt of her remarkable career, Diane waves to Times-Union Photographer Roberta Smith before taking her final plunge. Photos on pages 44, 45, 46 and 47 were taken by Miss Smith.

Still miles from her destination, Diane is seen at right in upper photo, stroking her way into the Long Island area of the lake. In lower photo she momentarily treads water while her pulse is taken. Such stops, however, were infrequent. Her pace was remarkably regular, interrupted only by waves whipped by winds.

MISSION ACCOMPLISHED!

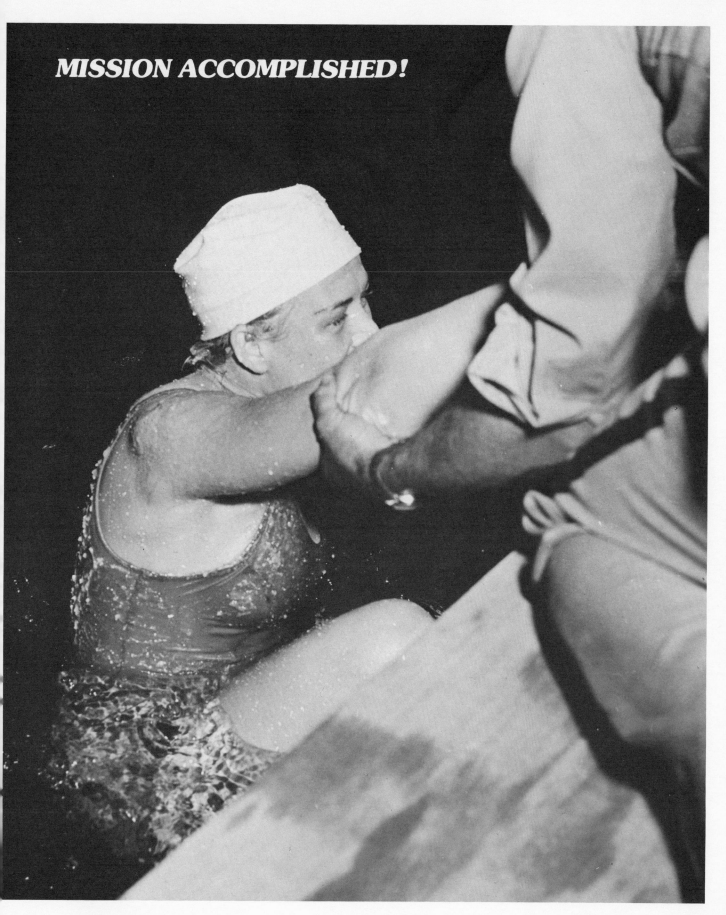

Willing hands grasp Diane's arms as she reaches her goal — the dock on the Beach Road at Lake George Village. The time: 10 p.m. She had been in the water for more than 35 hours after taking her initial plunge at the northern end at Ticonderoga.

Bounty Hunter

When New York State Began Paying
Bounties on Timber Wolves and
Panthers, George Muir created a
Record Never Equalled

Aerial photo of the Cranberry Lake region in the Northwestern Adirondacks, a favorite area of George Muir, greatest wolf and panther bounty hunter of them all. The lake, fed by the Oswegatchie River, was created in its present form by damming that river. In years gone by it was noted for its brook trout fishing. And famous personages, such as Frederic Remington, the artist, spent many Summers in the region.

Timber wolves. Sketch by the late Walter J. Schoonmaker.

They were famous or infamous. It all depends upon your ecological viewpoint.

But there were bounty hunters of sizable accomplishment in New York State's mountain region during the late 1800's and they were self contracted "hit" experts in the art of shooting or trapping off two species that will never return in number to prowl territorial domains once familiar to the spoors of past generations.

The early hunters most assuredly were not members of any "syndicate" dedicated to the elimination of all wildlife. They shot specific animals for the dollar bill. Some were strange, sometimes remarkable men; recluses in some instances, men torn between the desire to live the primitive life, yet faced with making a living from a more civilized and affluent one.

They were men born between two eras.

The moose and elk were never considered predators by early settlers. But they were sources of meat and hides for the hungry and needy, and trophies for the rich sports who shot everything in sight and then, surfeited with antlers, made such interesting furniture as chairs of horn to decorate their wilderness lodges.

The elk and the moose were, of course, shot out of existence.

The timber wolf and the panther, however, provoked nothing but anger, fear and retaliation; they were considered killers of such edible and productive commodities as sheep, fowl and other domestic stock. So was the Adirondack black bear, but the ubiquitous bruin never obtained the prominence of the wolf or panther in the mind of a growing population. Nor did it conjure visions of terror.

The dog-like creature which roamed the North County (Canis lupus occidentalis) was the timber wolf. Once it prowled the entire state. By 1899 it was, to all practical purposes, exterminated in all portions except the wildest areas of the Adirondacks, although a few, surprisingly, existed in counties outside the mountains.

The panther (Felis oregonensis hippolestes), the northeastern panther, went by many names. It was called the mountain lion, painter, puma or cougar. If the reader will scan the ship's manifest of furs reproduced in the introduction to this volume, he will notice they were also called "catts" by early inscribers.

Both the wolf and panther were creatures of the forest. Like the wolf, the panther by 1899 had been killed off except within the wildest regions.

How both managed to survive even up to this time is almost unbelievable. They were hunted relentlessly from earliest times. The Hessians of Burgoyne's army, marching to defeat at the Battle of Saratoga during the Revolution, had pets of wolf and panther cubs. Earlier, members of the garrison at Fort William Henry, during the French and Indian War, kept similar pets, killing them when they showed signs of maturity. In the early 1800's Sampson Paul, an Indian living on Diamond Island, Lake George, killed a panther while the animal was swimming. He used a fish spear. Whenever, wherever wolves or panthers were seen, they were objects destined for death.

In 1871 the State of New York in its wisdom decided there was no room for the predators. A bounty system was instituted. A panther brought the hunter $20. A wolf was worth $30. In those days that was quite a bit of money; a dollar went farther than Washington ever tossed it.

The $2,140 paid in bounties for panthers came from Saratoga, Essex, Hamilton, Franklin, Herkimer, Lewis and St. Lawrence Counties. The state paid $2,910 for timber wolves shot or trapped out of existence. The counties which produced these victims for the growing biological morgue included Broome, Essex, Franklin, Fulton, Hamilton, Herkimer, Lewis, Oneida, Otsego, St. Lawrence, Warren and Washington. Total killed up to the end of the period, 1897, was 98.

The total panther demise was 107. When one considers the size of areas controlled by individual beasts, this becomes a remarkable number. Unless as mates or families, the puma did not live side by side.

Reproductions of reports on bounty kills, containing the hunters, dates, towns, counties and amounts paid are contained in this chapter. They are from a New York State Museum Bulletin issued in 1899, Federick J.H. Merrill, Director. Analyze them. They are interesting. One realizes upsetting Nature's balance was a quick way to pick up a fast buck.

In analysis, the name of one man, George Muir, stands out unmistakably as the greatest bounty hunter of them all. Of 98 wolves killed for the money their carcasses brought, George Muir killed 39. Of 107 panthers extirpated, he killed 67.

His brother John, was a poor second in the Muir family; he killed only eight wolves and four panthers. George, therefore, unquestionably wears the crown. His wolf and panther kills were concentrated in the counties of Hamilton, St. Lawrence, Herkimer and Lewis. Interesting is that during a period of his hunting, the noted artist, Frederick Remington, was spending considerable time in the Cranberry Lake area of St. Lawrence County, building up his priceless collection. One doubts if the two ever met, however.

There were bounties paid on six wolves in the year 1897 when the records cease. Muir shot all six, four in Lewis County, the other two in St. Lawrence. He didn't round out the bounty program on panthers, however. In 1888 James Jagin, hunting near Wilmington Essex County, shot one, and in 1890, the last panther for which a bounty was paid in this period was killed by A.P. Flansburgh. In all places, he shot it in Saratoga County!

From 1891 to 1897 no lion was turned in for money. Perhaps some were shot, but it is doubtful. The $20 bounty would have brought the hunter forward.

Most unusual, if you analyze the bounty figures for wolves is the recorded fact that in all instances save two $30 was the amount paid individual hunters. But one wolf shot by George Muir in the Town of Fine, St.

The panther, or mountain lion of the Adirondacks, oddly enough, brought hunters only $20 each as compared to $30 offered for wolves. Yet the panther was every bit as capable a predator as the wolf.

Lawrence County on June 11, 1881, brought only $15. George Speare on August 17, 1871, killed two wolves in the Town of Hopkinton, St. Lawrence County; was given $30 for one and $15 for the other! No reason is given for the reductions.

The name of George Muir bothered me for some time after I first came across the state records. What kind of a man was he? Where did he hail from? He remains faceless insofar as I am concerned; I have come across no photograph of this gentleman. Which, of course, doesn't say one does not exist.

One day I began reading Herbert F. Keith's "Man of the Woods," published by Syracuse University Press and The Adirondack Museum in 1972. Mr. Keith is a remarkable man, 79, who lives in Wanakena. His book, one of early memories, offers a fascinating insight into the Cranberry Lake-Oswegatchie River region in St. Lawrence County. His style is extremely readable; his opinions pronounced. The book is a joy to read and reread, particularly for me, since I have canoed the area extensively.

Imagine my joyful surprise, therefore, after years of trying to find out something about George Muir, to suddenly see the name of this man in Mr. Keith's book. I called the author immediately. Did he know Muir personally?

He did indeed.

What kind of a man was he?

Muir, said Mr. Keith, came from Harrisville. He was about five-feet, seven-inches in height. He was of slender but muscular build. Unlike many Adirondack recluses, he wore no beard. He had a full head of hair. His eyesight was sharp.

Mr. Keith, a veteran of both World War One and Two, remembers seeing Muir about World War One time; Muir visited him occasionally at his Wanakena home, sometimes took advantage of an offer of a ride to Harrisville. Today Muir is buried at that community. He died at age 80, in the woods he loved and roamed so well; searchers found his snowshoes leaning against a tree. The body of the old man lay nearby.

The finding of Muir's body had its own kind of drama. Friends were unable to approach because Muir's German shepherd, Queenie, guarded her dead master. It was only when Wilfred Morrison, a guide who knew the dog well, spoke, that she relinquished the agony of guard duty.

They found her paws badly cut; her body emaciated from lack of food, for between the time Muir had succumbed and the time he was found she had made many trips back to Muir's isolated camp trying to get help — but always returned to the old man's body, fearful to leave it alone too long.

Muir, it might be explained, did his bounty hunting in his earlier years. In the later span of his life he became a caretaker for the Webb estate, living in a remote cabin on Gull Lake, west of the headwaters of the famed Oswegatchie River. He had camped at Gull for many years and when the Webb family purchased the huge

tract, it was stipulated Muir was to remain and in the employ of the family. His camp was 12 miles from Wanakena and eight miles from what was termed the estate's "main camp." One telephone line was the electronic umbilical cord connecting both.

Despite advancing years and diminished vigor Muir left the woods on occasion. During his 80th year he walked the 12 miles to Wanakena in the Spring, when the deep snows began to melt. On his return he was accompanied by Art Leary, an Oswegatchie River guide who had a camp six miles from Wanakena. Snowshoes were not used; an icy crust had formed and supported the men's weight. Leary's camp was reached and there both men rested and ate a solid meal. Muir, refreshed, said he would go on rather than stay the night, to take advantage of the crust. He departed.

The old man had promised to telephone his employer upon his arrival at Gull Lake. The call never came through. The search party was organized.

The job was difficult because Muir, seeking total privacy at his camp, had never marked a trail. Melting of snow had progressed to the point where tracking was impossible; streams were cresting and swamps overflowing. It was Wilfred Morrison who led searchers along possible routes and several sweeps, each over an expanding area, were made before the body was discovered.

In Mr. Keith's book, the end of Queenie is described thusly:

"Queenie was in bad shape after her long watch. A relative of George in another village was phoned. He did not want Queenie. He gave orders to shoot her."

Says Mr. Keith:

"Queenie was a beautiful German shepherd dog. I had known her for the nine years of her life. No dog ever served her master more faithfully, and no master loved his dog more than George did. As I went to see what was left of her, I wondered how such a faithful servant could be treated like this. I suddenly remembered something and looked at her right front paw. Yes, there was that large, deep scar which had only recently healed. The other paws showed signs of being cut from running on the Spring's icy crust for many miles."

Thus the end of the career of probably the greatest bounty hunter of them all, deep in the woods, a lonely death save for the presence of a companion with no power of speech, no means of communication save that which she could devise in her own faithful way.

Thus, too, the end of a dog whose world came suddenly to an explosive, terrifying end.

(Bounty figures on following pages)

51

BOUNTY PAYMENTS ON PANTHERS

Table of bounties paid for panthers in New York under law of 1871

County	Town	Date	By whom killed	Amount paid
Essex	Newcomb	10 N 1871	J. C. Fanner...........	$20
"	"	11 D 1871	"	20
"	"	"	"	20
"	"	"	"	20
"		25 F 1880	W. H. Cullen	20
"	Wilmington	14 Jl 1883	Arthur Croninshield and J. C. Sanders...	20
"	"	11 Ag 1883	" ...	20
"	"	14 Ag 1888	James Jagins	20
Franklin	Dickinson	4 D 1872	M. H. Ober	20
"	"	29 Ag 1873	C. A. Merrill	20
Hamilton	Lake Pleasant...	29 F 1872	A. B. Sturges & B. Page	20
"	Long Lake	29 F 1878	J. W. Schultz.........	20
"	"	21 Je 1882	George Muir	20
"	"	"	"	20
"	"	22 Jl 1882	"	20
"	"	24 Jl 1882	"	20
"	"	10 S 1882	"	20
"	"	28 O 1883	"	20
"	"	"	"	20
"	"	30 N 1883	"	20
"	"	5 F 1887	"	20
"	"	8 F 1887	"	20
"	Wells	19 D 1876	Silas Call	20
Herkimer	Wilmurt.........	11 D 1877	E. L. Sheppard	20
"	"	12 D 1877	"	20
"	"	13 D 1877	"	20
"	"	26 F 1878	E. N. Arnold..........	20
"	"	8 Mar 1878	"	20
"	"	26 D 1878	A. S. Marshall	20
"	"	"	"	20
"	"	25 O 1882	George Muir	20
"	"	30 N 1882	"	20
"	"	10 My 1883	"	20
"	"	"	"	20
"	"	2 Ag 1883	"	20
"	"	"	"	20
"	"	8 Ja 1884	"	20
"	"	19 Ja 1884	"	20
Lewis	Croghan	20 N 1882	"	20
"	"	25 Je 1883	"	20
"	"	29 F 1884	"	20
"	Diana	23 My 1882	"	20
"	"	10 Jc 1882	"	20
"	"	28 Je 1882	"	20
"	"	13 Jl 1882	"	20
"	"	18 Ag 1882	"	20
"	"	"	"	20

BOUNTY PAYMENTS ON PANTHERS

Table of bounties paid for panthers in New York under law of 1871, continued

County	Town	Date	By whom killed	Amount paid
Lewis	Diana	14 My 1883	George Muir	$20
"	"	5 Je 1883	"	20
"	"	12 Jl 1883	"	20
"	"	"	"	20
"	"	5 F 1884	"	20
"	"	"	"	20
"	"	25 Ap 1884	"	20
"	"	"	"	20
"	"	18 Mar 1885	"	20
"	"	2 Ap 1885	"	20
"	"	1 Mar 1886	"	20
"	"	10 Mar 1886	"	20
"	"	25 Ap 1886	"	20
"	"	5 My 1886	"	20
Saratoga	Day	3 O 1887	L. J. De Long	20
"	"	6 Ja 1890	A. P. Flansburgh	20
St Lawrence	Canton	15 F 1878	Hiram Hutchins	20
"	Colton	23 N 1880	"	20
"	"	15 Ja 1881	"	20
"	Fine	7 Je 1871	S. B. Ward	20
"	"	22 Je 1871	"	20
"	"	"	"	20
"	"	15 Je 1871	John Muir	20
"	"	26 Je 1871	"	20
"	"	29 Je 1871	"	20
"	"	23 O 1872	Henry Marsh	20
"	"	8 Je 1873	John Muir	20
"	"	24 Ja 1877	Webster Pastlow	20
"	"	1 My 1879	George Muir	20
"	"	15 Je 1880	"	20
"	"	26 Ap 1881	"	20
"	"	23 My 1881	"	20
"	"	16 Jl 1881	"	20
"	"	26 Ag 1881	"	20
"	"	10 S 1881	"	20
"	"	"	"	20
"	"	6 O 1881	"	20
"	"	7 O 1881	"	20
"	"	7 N 1881	"	20
"	Hopkinton	19 N 1873	N. A. Gale	20
"	"	4 N 1874	N. E. Wait	20
"	"	26 D 1876	C. N. Gale	20
"	"	12 O 1879	Peter Brosseau	20
"	Parishville	24 O 1875	Michael Duffy	20
"	Pitcairn	21 Je 1883	George Muir	20
"	"	22 Je 1883	"	20
"	"	22 Jl 1883	"	20
"	"	"	"	20
"	"	15 S 1883	"	20
"	"	23 D 1883	"	20
"	"	"	"	20
"	"	21 Mar 1884	"	20
"	"	1 D 1884	"	20
"	"	26 Ja 1885	"	20
"	"	27 Mar 1885	"	20
"	"	28 Mar 1885	"	20
"	"	15 My 1885	"	20
"	"	23 My 1885	"	20
"	"	25 Ap 1886	"	20
"	Township No. 11	24 O 1871	Michael Duffy	20

Summary by counties

County	Number killed	Amount paid
Essex	8	$160
Franklin	2	40
Hamilton	13	260
Herkimer	15	300
Lewis	23	460
Saratoga	2	40
St Lawrence	44	880
Total	107	$2 140

Summary by years

Year	Number killed	Amount paid
1871	8	$160
1872	6	120
1873	3	60
1874	1	20
1875	1	20
1876	2	40
1877	4	80
1878	6	120
1879	2	40
1880	3	60
1881	10	200
1882	14	280
1883	21	420
1884	9	180
1885	7	140
1886	5	100
1887	3	60
1888	1	20
1889	0	....
1890	1	20
1891	0	....
1892	0	....
1893	0	....
1894	0	....
1895	0	....
1896	0	....
1897	0	....
Total	107	$2 140

BOUNTY PAYMENTS ON WOLVES

Table of bounties paid for wolves in New York under law of 1871

County	Town	Date	By whom killed	Amount paid
Broome	Barker	23 F 1881	B. H. Moak	$30
Essex	Minerva	6 S 1872	Wesley Rice	30
"	"	"	"	30
"	"	25 Jl 1885	Samuel Wilson	30
Franklin	Brandon	12 Je 1875	Calvin Wait	30
"	"	17 Je 1875	"	30
"	Duane	4 Jl 1874	J. H. Bean	30
Fulton	Bleecker	10 Ap 1895	E. Kosobuske	30
Hamilton	Long Lake	28 Mar 1882	Peter Fahlgren	30
"	"	1 Ap 1882	"	30
"	"	27 S 1882	George Muir	30
"	"	25 Mar 1883	"	30
"	"	17 Ja 1887	J. H. Higbey	30
"	Wells	16 Mar 1883	Peter Decker	30
"	"	"	"	30
Herkimer	Ohio	28 Ja 1882	Henry Sheldon	30
"	"	"	"	30
"	Wilmurt	8 Jl 1883	George Muir	30
Lewis	Batchfordville	10 N 1881	Frank Riley	30
"	Diana	27 Je 1882	George Muir	30
"	"	27 Ap 1884	"	30
"	"	10 My 1895	"	30
"	"	18 My 1895	"	30
"	"	18 Ap 1896	"	30
"	"	16 S 1896	"	30
"	"	22 O 1896	"	30
"	"	20 D 1896	"	30
"	"	7 Ja 1897	"	30
"	"	31 My 1897	"	30
"	"	5 Ag 1897	"	30
"	"	23 S 1897	"	30
"	Greig	10 N 1881	George Botchford	30
"	Lyonsdale	4 O 1882	John Camp	30
"	"	13 O 1882	"	30
"	"	17 N 1882	"	30
"	"	15 D 1882	Thomas Lee	30
Oneida	Floyd	8 F 1886	W. A. & I. E. Bennett.	30
"	Forestport	14 F 1882	Henry Durrin	30
"	"	15 Mar 1882	"	30
"	"	19 Mar 1882	"	30
"	"	2 Ap 1882	Daniel Rodgers	30
"	"	9 Ap 1882	"	30
"	"	14 O 1882	Henry Durrin & S. L. Fones	30
"	"	19 O 1882	Henry Durrin & S. L. Fones	30
"	"	18 D 1882	Henry Durrin	30
Otsego	Plainfield	14 F 1888	J. D. Wilkinson	30

55

Table of bounties paid for wolves in New York under law of 1871, continued

County	Town	Date		By whom killed	Amount paid
St Lawrence..	Brasher	21 D	1872	Timothy Desmond	$30
" ..	Clifton	8 Je	1895	George Muir	30
" ..	"	10 S	1895	"	30
" ..	"	18 S	1895	"	30
" ..	"	1 S	1896	"	30
" ..	"	30 O	1896	"	30
" ..	"	15 O	1897	"	30
" ..	"	30 N	1897	"	30
" ..	Colton	5 N	1880	Abram Barkley.........	30
" ..	Fine	17 O	1871	John Muir	30
" ..	"	26 My	1872	"	30
" ..	"	7 N	1872	"	30
" ..	"	22 My	1875	"	30
" ..	"	24 My	1875	"	30
" ..	"	15 My	1876	"	30
" ..	"	5 My	1877	"	30
" ..	"	14 Jl	1877	"	30
" ..	"	8 Ap	1878	George Muir	30
" ..	"	16 S	1878	"	30
" ..	"	29 Ap	1879	"	30
" ..	"	26 Ap	1880	"	30
" ..	"	3 O	1880	"	30
" ..	"	28 Ap	1881	"	30
" ..	"	23 My	1881	"	30
" ..	"	11 Je	1881	"	15
" ..	"	"		"	30
" ..	"	20 Jl	1881	"	30
" ..	"	24 Ag	1881	"	30
" ..	"	28 S	1881	"	30
" ..	"	8 N	1881	"	30
" ..	Fowler	7 Je	1888	W. S. Clark.........	30
" ..	Hopkinton	17 Ag	1871	George Speare.........	30
" ..	"	"		"	15
" ..	"	6 O	1871	Joseph Whitney.......	30
" ..	"	9 O	1876	George Peck	30
" ..	"	6 N	1880	Jonathan Baldwin	30
" ..	"	13 N	1880	H. C. Hibbard	30
" ..	"	20 S	1881	"	30
" ..	Parishville	13 N	1880	"	30
" ..	Pitcairn.........	4 N	1872	Aaron Thomas	30
" ..	"	12 D	1873	"	30
" ..	"	1 N	1884	Geore Muir.........	30
" ..	"	26 Je	1885	"	30
" ..	"	4 Jl	1885	"	30
" ..	"	10 Ap	1886	"	30
Warren	Thurman.........	10 F	1883	Roland Gamby.........	30
"	"	14 F	1883	"	30
Washington ..	Dresden.........	10 Mar	1882	"	30
" ..	"	"		"	30
" ..	"	3 Ag	1882	"	30
" ..	"	3 Mar	1883	"	30
" ..	Kingsbury.........	17 Ja	1883	William Casey	30
" ..	"	24 F	1883	Samuel Ferris.........	30

BOUNTY PAYMENTS ON WOLVES

Summary by counties

County	Number killed	Amount paid
Broome	1	$30
Essex	3	90
Franklin	3	90
Fulton	1	30
Hamilton	7	210
Herkimer	3	90
Lewis	18	540
Oneida	9	270
Otsego	1	30
St Lawrence	45	1 335
Warren	1	30
Washington	6	180
Total	98	$2 910

Summary by years

Year	Number killed	Amount paid
1871	4	$105
1872	6	180
1873	1	30
1874	1	30
2875	4	120
1876	2	60
1877	2	60
1878	2	60
1879	1	30
1880	6	180
1881	12	345
1882	21	630
1883	9	270
1884	2	60
1885	2	60
1886	2	60
1887	1	30
1888	2	60
1889	0	....
1890	0	....
1891	0	....
1892	0	....
1893	0	....
1894	0	....
1895	6	180
1896	6	180
1897	6	180
Total	98	$2 910

57

Wizard of
the Wheel

Undeniable is the fact that some Canadian drivers have alarming skills which at times defy comprehension. On Route 28 one day while driving to Indian Lake to visit Conservation Officer Jack Carroll, two of the Friendly Neighbors became impatient with the sedate pace I usually maintain in this beautiful area.

So they passed.

This in itself would not be unusual except for two simple facts. Route 28 between North River and Indian Lake is a two lane highway. I occupied one. And both Canadians passed me abreast of each other, holding positions with the precision of trained chariot horses.

Many lawmen who patrol highways in the wilderness area will tell you the Canadian who wheels his way with cheerful vigor through the Adirondacks is in an exclusive class. If roadless Mt. Marcy is ever to be climbed by car, there is no question some gas powered Canadian Marco Polo will be the first to do so. One of these days a Canadian will register as the first 46'er who climbed the highest peaks by gear instead of foot. It would not be surprising.

Take Charbot Germain, for instance. He did what no other driver, Canadian or otherwise (and that includes pilots from New Jersey and Connecticut also famous for driving habits) has done since the Adirondacks decided to become mountains. He tried the impossible and accomplished it.

He drove a 65-foot tractor trailer, weighing tons, three-and-one-half miles on a snowmobile trail, following what he hoped was a "short cut" to Utica!

To compound this miracle of transportation the feat was accomplished during darkness.

It was to be an extraordinary day that Saturday, Dec. 15, 1973, when the young man, seeking directions to Utica, was told to take the "short cut" by leaving the Northway at the North Creek exit and then hitting Route 8. The only difficulty was that Charbot absorbed only part of the message. His knowledge of English was fragmentary and his best effort in trying to explain anything in that language was to describe it in French. His mind netted the word "Creek," but "North" dropped through the mesh. Eventually, and nobody seems to know quite how, he found himself in Stony Creek.

Now a driver on his way to Utica with a tractor trailer can easily make up his mind that somewhere along the line a turn or two had eluded him. But not Charbot. He took the road to Harrisburg Lake, which dead ends at that isolated body of water. There is a highway sign in Stony Creek which announces this interesting fact, but Charbot either didn't understand or missed it in the growing darkness of 6 p.m.

At this point the highway, if one can call it that, leaves its identity as Dr. Jekyll and becomes Mr. Hyde. It is known as the old "Bakerstown Road." It is of ancient vintage, once upon a time a town road that originally snaked its way through wilderness to Hope Falls. Today any professional football team which used it in broken field practice could win the Super Bowl with ease. It was abandoned more than a half century ago. It is unpaved. It has the undulations of a belly dancer. It is eroded, filled with boulders and an aggressive Mother Nature has made several attempts to return it to her primeval womb. It is a hiking and snowmobile trail.

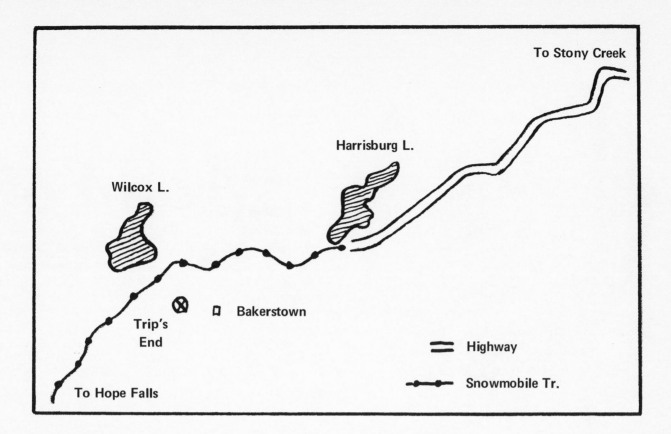

Wilcox L.

Harrisburg L.

To Stony Creek

⊗ Trip's End

▢ Bakerstown

Highway

Snowmobile Tr.

To Hope Falls

Assistant District Forest Ranger Charles Severance of North Creek says it can be traveled by a four wheel drive vehicle "if one doesn't care much for the vehicle." It is one wheel track wide. It is, in effect, a passageway through the Dead Sea of the wilderness and the forest has the hungry look of walls of water.

"I can vouch," says Severance, "it is one hell of a road."

Charbot, comfortable in the heated cab of his personally owned, $28,000 tractor, was undaunted; with the empty rig singing its song of squeaks, grunts and groans, he crossed the narrow causeway at Harrisburg Lake and took off on the Bakerstown Road. At Utica he was scheduled to pick up a load of horses. Presumably they were to be returned to Canada for slaughter.

"What he was thinking of when he started climbing over the boulders and going through the mudholes with brush and tree limbs dragging over his windshield, I don't know," comments Severance. "But it didn't faze him. He kept right on going."

To top off the scene there was about a two inch cover of wet snow. Through total darkness, the trail ahead pinpointed only by headlights, Charbot drove his way. If the total absence of oncoming traffic proved of interest, it was not noted. If the absence of habitation was noted, it meant nothing. He was a determined man, this Canadian, and he had a job to do.

Charbot moved an astonishing three-and-one-half miles on this path of grease. Then he hit a grade his rig couldn't climb because of lack of traction. He applied his brakes. The tractor trailer slid backwards and jackknifed. To add to the misery of the moment, a boulder had knocked off a fuel line fitting and the tractor engine developed a pronounced stutter. It also started to rain.

Says Severance:

"So there he was, to hell and gone, out in the boondocks, miles from the nearest house, in pitch black, and getting colder than hell. He went back to two hunting camps, tried to get in, but both were locked and though he easily could have broken in he made no attempt to do so. He spent the night crouched in his cab in a foreign land and almost froze. The engine was running so poorly he couldn't get any heat."

There Charbot remained all day Sunday in a downpour. Rescue came in the form of a group traveling by Jeep from Harrisburg Lake. Nobody aboard could quite believe their eyes at the huge apparition. It took time for the scene to sink in. But they rescued the soaked and chattering Charbot, drove him to the nearest Forest Ranger, Lynn Day, in Stony Creek, and Lynn got some dry clothes on his visitor, filled him full of hot food and called upon the good services of a local lady, Virginia Lorraine, who spoke and understood French. She got Charbot's story, found him a room for the night.

Ranger Day got busy on the phone. On Monday at 8 a.m. a small expedition was on its way to the rubber shod brontosaurus immobilized in the woods. In the lead were Lou and Tom Fisher, two of Day's fire wardens, with an International 500 bulldozer and some chain. Lynn and Charbot followed in Lynn's truck, and Rangers Mike Hagadorn and Severance brought up the rear. Mike, who speaks French fluently, served as interpreter.

Deep in the woods, in rain and wet snow, a bulldozer clears an area so truck trailer can be lined up with the snowmobile trail.

This is the truly astonishing scene which met the party from Wilcox Lake. Photo shows empty trailer at total right angle to trail. Polaroid pictures by Chuck Severance.

Nobody could have dreamed up the scene as it existed. The Fisher boys knew just what to do. "They bulled, shoved and cajoled the trailer around until they could get the tractor unhooked and up the hill and out of the way," Severance recounts.

Then the Fishers leveled the trailer, firmed up the mud beneath with stone and logs, and rehooked it to the tractor. With tractor and trailer thus joined once again in familiar and raucous embrace, the whole thing was towed to a clearing where everyone took a breather. It had been hard, demanding, difficult work, under the most brutal of circumstances. And all this time, of course, says Severance, Mike Hagadorn was passing on orders in French to Charbot.

"It sounded like the Fulton Fish Market and looked like it too, with all the arm waving and gesticulating!"

At Harrisburg Lake the tractor engine stuttered its final gasp, quit cold. The Fisher boys finally got the fuel line repaired and Charbot patched a radiator hose. That was all the damage the rig suffered.

Adirondack fairness and hospitality, evidenced throughout the entire episode, didn't end at this point. The Fishers had Charbot at their mercy; they could have financially skinned him alive and thrown him into total dismay. But Lou and Tom Fisher aren't built that way. They merely charged him their regular bulldozer rate.

There is interesting commentary as a follow-up to this amazing story. As mentioned, the trailer was used to transport horses. Charbot was not a dealer; he hauled the animals. But the subject of handling the animals had, by the Fall of 1973, become a touchy subject in the North Country. There had been examples of cruelty in transportation, particularly on the Northway, and North Country SPCA's were up in arms. Out of curiosity, Severance examined the trailer itself. It belonged to what he calls "one of those infamous horse traders that the State Troopers have been stopping on the Northway."

His comment:

"After examining the trailer I can see why 'infamous' is a mild word. This particular trailer had a galvanized tin liner on the inside from the bed of the trailer to about four feet high, which had been torn and ripped so there were literally HUNDREDS of jagged edges that certainly had to lacerate and mangle some of the horses usually jammed into it. What a bloody mess those horses must be when unloaded at the slaughterhouse.

"I have no doubt that the killing of old and worn-out horses is a legitimate business. They eventually would have to be dispensed somehow. But certainly any animal under the control of a human being should have the right to a humane death not preceded by a traumatic, terror-ridden ride in a jammed trailer. Those guilty should be soundly horse whipped and then shot."

* * *

An after note: The Bakerstown Road was not only the scene of the above happenstance. Other strange things have occurred. During the black fly season in 1973 a young girl, driving a convertible, drove much less distance on the snowmobile trail. When finally her car got hung up on a boulder, the car top had been ripped to shreds. She was bitten from head to foot by the blood hungry miniature monsters.

When the girl was found, rescuers were slightly taken aback. And for good reason. She was dressed only in a bikini.

Adirondack Wildlife

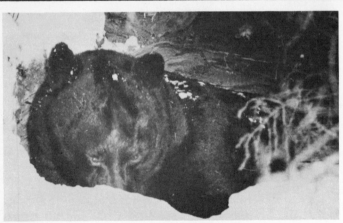

As the supreme animal, master of all, Man has been around a long time; evidence of his Stone Age culture in New York State has been found dating back at least 70,000 years. Man was in this State using stone tools at the same time the bushy-browed Neanderthal was gnawing bones in Europe and parts of Africa.

Man wasn't alone.

Living side by side with him was an astonishing array of animals, many of them carnivores, big enough, ferocious enough to delight any hunter of today with his high powered rifle.

In prehistoric days, for instance, behemoths such as the mammoth and mastodon once roamed the Adirondack region. Remains of these giants have been found in Lewis County as well as southern Warren County. In Jefferson County remains of the musk ox have been excavated. In Clinton County evidence of the prehistoric elk and seal has been found. Caribou once roamed the State; remains have been found as far south as Schenectady County, in the sand and gravel of glacial Lake Albany.

Buffalo, with a horn spread of six feet, existed, and those great natural engineers, beaver, swam and built their dams in the streams of the day. They were twice the size of today's animals. The Adirondack black bear was the size of the grizzly; one estimate is the beast weighed in at 1,500 pounds. The heaviest black bear in modern times was live-trapped for tagging near Tupper Lake and weighed just over 600 pounds. Moose and elk were common. So was the whitetail.

The wolverine, ferocity incorporated, was present and so was the wild pig. Astonishingly, so was the horse. If men of those ancient days caught them, it wasn't for the ride. They ate them.

No authentic dinosaur remains have been found in the State. Which, of course, doesn't mean the giants didn't prowl the area. The age of the dinosaur was an estimated 60,000,000 years ago. They did leave evidence, but in stone; dinosaur tracks have been found not in New York State, but along the Connecticut River. But if they existed there, can there be doubt they once moved in the Adirondack area of that dim age?

The Ice Age is only thousands of years distant. Some say today all of us are living in an intermediate period; there will be another. But Nature moves slowly and none of us will be around to see it. If it does occur, perhaps evolution will develop new kinds of animals, to cope with new conditions. Man may live in heated and enclosed cities or he may just grow fur and web-toed, snowshoe feet.

In historic times the State and the Adirondacks continued as a stronghold of animal life. The beaver was plentiful but because its pelt suited fashion, it was hunted to such an extent it became rare in the North Country; the capture in the 1880's of one live beaver "on the Raquette River between Upper Saranac and Big Tupper's Lake about a mile below the Sweeney Carry" was unusual enough to be recorded. The wolverine ranged in these days but in 1899 had almost vanished; some reports specified they lived in the Raquette Lake section. In earlier years they were found farther south; one was killed in Rensselaer County in 1811. The wolverine no longer is native to the Adirondacks.

In all probability, the buffalo did not roam the hill country. It is believed the buffalo, as we know it today, did penetrate into the State from the West as far as Syracuse. But no remains have been found in the Adirondacks, not even the southern fringes.

Seals were common in the Upper St. Lawrence and in the mid 1880's one reportedly was shot and killed while resting on an ice floe in Lake Champlain, near Crown Point, Essex County. One instance is even more remarkable. A seal was shot in Onondaga Lake, Syracuse area, in 1882. No lake in the State has seals today. They are sometimes sighted in the lower Hudson and one a few years ago managed to reach Albany where it died, soaked and poisoned by industrial wastes and oil.

The moose, once freely hunted in the Adirondacks, is long gone, although an occasional Marco Polo of the species is sighted wandering through. The panther and timber wolf are only memories. The big game today is the black bear and the whitetail.

The fisher, or "black cat," was once thought to be extinct, but has returned. The Canada lynx, also thought a goner, occasionally is seen. Bobcats are common today.

The mink exists today and so does the otter. The muskrat, the "musquash," long ago adapted itself to Man and survives without difficulty. In prehistoric days the fox existed. It remains as an Adirondack animal. The coyote has replaced the timber wolf and is now considered a pest by many, along with the snowmobile.

Whether the skunk wafted its weaponry in the dawn of history is not known, but this animal is very much part of the Adirondack scene. The opossum, a marsupial, moved into New York State about the time of the Civil War and has remained ever since. The porcupine remains despite intensive killing.

The small game hunter seeks the cottontail and the European hare and the squirrel. He hunts the raccoon and on occasion a trapper will find a golden eagle gripped by claws of the trap instead of the fur bearing animal he seeks. The American, or bald eagle, once common, is uncommon and widespread use of pesticides has been blamed for its elimination and elimination of other members of the hawk family.

The magnificent elk of historic times no longer exists and efforts to restock this big member of the deer family have failed. The wild boar is not native to the Adirondacks, but in the early 1900's some were stocked and eventually vanished. Within the past few years, in the Sabael region around Indian Lake, a small herd of wild boar was found, thus astonishing everyone in the area.

Some were shot and live-trapped. A few are at the Bronx Zoo today. It is believed they were deliberately and secretly brought into the Indian Lake section and released by someone wishing a more exotic type of creature. Adirondackers, however, reacted swiftly.

The weasel is with us and so is the marten.

Perhaps, with true wilderness areas now established in the Adirondack Forest Preserve, the moose, the panther, the timber wolf may return. If so, they should be left alone.

In 1842 the known New York mammals totaled 56. By the turn of the century the number had risen to 81. But this number included not only small and big game, but varieties of squirrels, moles, mice, shrews — and even the porpoise, a sea beast, hardly an Adirondack native.

The future of animal life in the Adirondacks is strictly up to Man. He's the manager. Over-hunting, such as in the form of the so-called doe permit, which allowed killing of whitetail incubators, shows up in the lessening of the deer population. Snowmobile harrassment of animals in the Winter is hardly conducive to perpetuation of any species. Pollution is as deadly as a gun.

All of us have, in the North Country, a vast sanctuary of life which in the past has been misused and abused. It is our job today to maintain that sanctuary, to enjoy what we have, not to find it necessary to live on memories of what once existed.

MR. MONKEY MITTS — THE RACCOON

ARE CHILDREN AND ANIMALS ALIKE?
THESE COMPARISONS MAY JUST PROVE A POINT

MR. MONKEY MITTS
CAN BE PLAYFUL AND CUTE

A busy raccoon is a tired raccoon. And sleep comes in many poses. Top: A tired youngster shields his eye from the sun while he takes an Instant Snooze. Sometimes the dog, owned by the author, and the 'coon slept together. When they did, the dog's rump was always handy as a pillow. In this instance, the raccoon is too busy watching the camera to get any shut eye.

BUT THE MASKED ROBBER
CAN BE DESTRUCTIVE AT TIMES

Life and death struggle, photographed over a period of time. Top left: a phoebe looks over a nesting site and at top right, her home completed, she sits contentedly on eggs. Later a prowling, hungry raccoon scares her off. Photo at left shows start of his house-wrecking abilities. This was one instance where the time-honored habit of "washing" food didn't appeal to the bird watching masked robber.

Dramatically, aggressively and mercilessly, while the mother phoebe twitters helplessly in a nearby tree, the raccoon begins to rip the nest apart. At left: Having completed his destruction, he pushes nest off its foundation beam, then peers curiously at the scene below. What remained? Only a portion of the nest and fragments of egg shells. Result: One phoebe without a family, one raccoon with egg on his face.

BUSHEL OF FUN —
BASKET OF TROUBLE

Bears are not true hibernators. Unexpected visitors during cold Winter months can awaken them. Here is graphic proof as Joe Howard shines a flashlight beam on an obviously perplexed and suspicious bear in its Winter den. Photo is by Nick Drahos. Bears, incidentally, do not always seek natural caves for Winter sleep. Some actually create nesting areas and "maternity wards" in windfalls.

Here is an example of a bear's Winter pad in comparatively open territory, near Schuyler Falls, Clinton County. The mother, disturbed by a hunter, abandoned her two cubs, including the one at left. Both were raised for approximately three months by the author. Estimated age of the youngster shown is about one month. Hair on this cub had all the qualities of a brush of steel wire and, one might add, the cub had the lung power of a power mower on a quiet Sunday morning. And used it frequently!

How big is a month old cub? Not too big indeed. The helpless critter above rests flat on its belly alongside a pack of king-sized cigarettes. The reason: No leg power. However one month later the same cub is shown perfectly capable of standing — and judging from the size of its claws, doing a bang-up job of scratching!

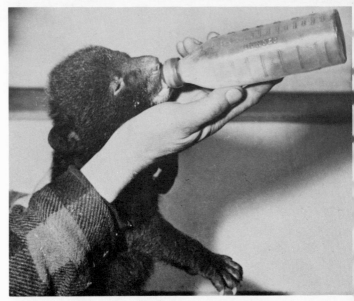

An armful of healthy Adirondack bear cubs is no easy bundle to hold as the expression on the youngster's face proves. One of the reasons is the presence (indisputable when cubs are frisky) of 40 remarkably sharp claws. These cubs were fed milk and syrup when very young, gradually were introduced to an added diet of ground meat, cereals and fruits as they grew older. Other photos are self explanatory. In the lower one you are looking at a forepaw. Imagine this magnified many times when the animal becomes an adult and you can easily envision why the blow of a bear is a fearsome, devastating thing.

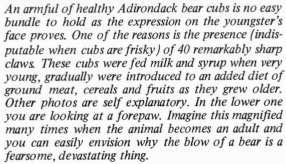

Bear cubs, being young, curious and frisky, often wander. This excellent painting by Clayt Seagears, former head of the Division of Conservation Education for New York State, and an internationally known artist and zoologist, portrays an unexpected meeting between cub and otter. Confrontation is on a rock where the otter often feeds. Startled cub drawn from life with one of cubs raised by author as model. Painting used through courtesy of the Conservationist Magazine.

Two examples of bear signs in the woods. At left is what is known as a "bear beech." The bear, in climbing the tree for its nuts, leaves claw wounds on the bark, which heal black, leaving a visible "trail" on its trunk. This was snapped on Gore Mountain at North Creek. But any beech grove will show similar signs. In second photo, taken at the Pack Forest, Warrensburg, sign is evident in this rotten log, shredded by a bear hungry for grubs.

Next Page: Another Winter den, near Raquette Lake, in a windfall. Arrow points to sleeping bear, a black mass from a distance. That's Conservation Officer Jack Carroll of Indian Lake at left and friend Gordie Aldous at right. Bear's breathing was clocked at four times a minute. When awakened, it raised its head slowly (lower photo) for an initial sleepy-eyed glance at the "awakening party."

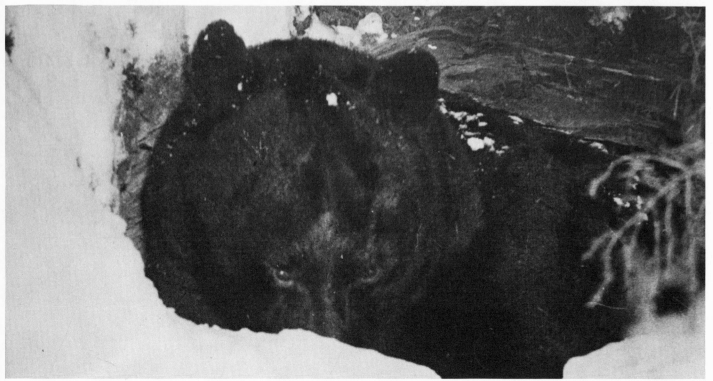

Before the big male on the preceding page closed his eyes and returned to his dormant state, there was one more opportunity to "shoot" him with a Speed Graphic. This time, his head was fully exposed and his brain was starting to function. The bear was estimated at about 400 pounds. The den was reached on snowshoes; snow depth when the author took this photo, was approximately six to seven feet and the time mid Winter.

BUT BEARS CAN BE DANGEROUS

Aftermath of midnight raid. Around midnight Conservation Officer Jack Carroll and Mrs. Carroll of Indian Lake heard their Brittany spaniel barking in the kitchen. There was good reason. Looking down upon their rear porch by flashlight, the Carrolls spotted this huge black bear, obviously irritated at the dog's frantic barking, attempting to gain violent entrance into their home.

While Mrs. Carroll held the light, her husband ended the animal's attempt at entry with a well placed shot. This was the scene the following morning as children gathered 'round to gaze in awe at the size of bruin. The chain around the animal's neck was attached to a small truck. That much power was needed to drag the carcass off the porch. Photo furnished through courtesy of the Carroll family.

THE WHITETAIL

Harsh Winters, dog and coyote predations, lack of food and highway kills can raise deer herd mortality in any area to serious proportions. Replenishment is needed. That means fawns. The one pictured on the preceding page was photographed in the North Creek area. These triplets are not Adirondack fawns, but typical of the whitetail, which ranges throughout the state. Triplets are being restrained by Conservation Officer John Bouck, then stationed at Middleburg, Schoharie County; they show infinite grace and delicacy of the young. These fawns were orphaned.

Orphaned whitetail young are sometimes "adopted" by those who find them, a practice discouraged by the State Department of Environmental Conservation. But between the time the animals are found and the time they are turned over to the department, interesting developments may occur. Like raiding a bread box. Lower photo might be entitled "Survival of the fittest." In this case, the fawn, spotting the baby's bottle of milk, seems to be the winner!

An adult male, still in "velvet," is startled by the camera flash of the late Walter J. Schoonmaker. Eventually the velvety cover of the antlers will be rubbed off and the male is ready to take on all comers during the mating, or "rutting" season. At left is a shed antler, found by Mr. Schoonmaker on Tongue Mountain, Lake George. When the combat season is over and life returns to normalcy, the bucks shed racks naturally. Mice and porcupines find them a rich source of calcium. They eat them.

During Spring, Summer and Fall deer roam freely unless scattered into other areas by dogs, coyotes or when upheavals such as logging operations occur on their range. In the Winter the animals "yard up" in a sheltered spot. These photos, as well as the one at the top of the next page, were taken by Walter J. Schoonmaker. Note pathways worn in limited yard excursions. Bottom photo, next page, shows John Beals inspecting length of leap of a deer, frightened in the Boquet River region. Measured leap: Fourteen feet! Photo, taken by the author, snapped before yarding had occurred.

As seen on the preceding page, the leaping power of the whitetail is extraordinary. Here are two more examples to prove the point. They were taken by Tom Sheehan, former Times-Union photographer, now a cameraman with WRGB-TV, Schenectady. This buck, still in velvet, was a comparatively tame animal which frequented a farm. At left, it vaults a fence easily from a standing start, while in other photo its leap out of a stall is done with equal ease and grace.

Never is death far distant. The buck in the top photo was killed near Blue Mountain Lake by one of the greatest of deer predators, the automobile. Other photo: All that remains of what once was graceful life is this carcass. The deer was chased into exhaustion by a dog pack during Winter and its hindquarters literally ripped apart before it died in agony in the Schroon Lake area. Dogs are a constant menace in late Winter when deer are at their weakest. This photo was furnished by the late Conservation Officer Dwinal Kerste.

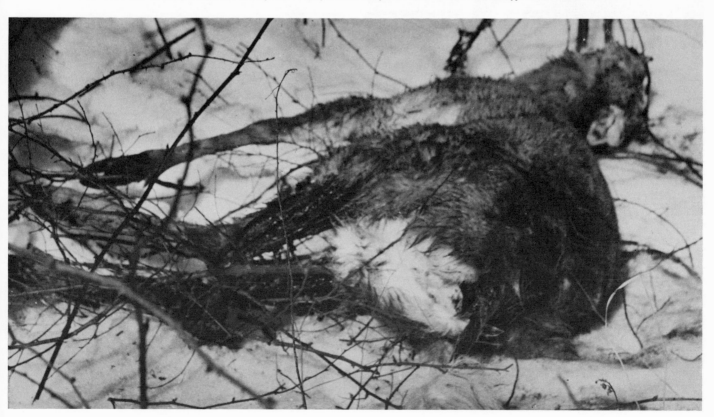

THE OPOSSUM

The opossum, despite some reports, is no new stranger to New York State; one was captured in Essex County in 1885! This unusual animal which wandered into the State from southern climes, is a marsupial; that is, it carries its young in a stomach pouch. It may on occasion "play possum," feigning death when threatened, but it is also known as a fighter. It is, despite its appearance, perfectly capable of surviving harsh New York State Winters. One reason, perhaps, other than its fur, is that it will eat almost anything.

THE ELK

The elk, or Wapiti, once roamed the Adirondacks but has long been shot out of existence; the last recorded kill was in the Minerva area in 1946. Efforts have been made to re-stock this member of the deer family in the Adirondacks but have failed. This mature male, still in velvet, was photographed by Walter J. Schoonmaker in the Yellowstone Park area. The photo of the bull moose, on the next page, also taken by Schoonmaker, shows the animal's rack dripping water as it raises its head with a mouthful of underwater plants. The moose is a vanished species insofar as the Adirondacks are concerned, but occasionally one may wander in and out of the Park area.

THE COYOTE

Where the coyote, sometimes called the "brush wolf" came from is anybody's guess. Some say Canada; others say the animal was brought into New York State by travelers from the West who carried them as pets. At any rate, the animal is now an established predator in the Adirondacks. When the bounty system was in effect, the late Fred Streever of Northwest Bay, Lake George, author, breeder of fox hounds and builder of primitively styled homes, hunted them frequently, found many in the Stony Creek area. Here he poses with one specimen, weight about 40 pounds.

More examples of predators in the North Country. Photo at top was taken of hunters and their coyote kill in the hill country west of Lake George. What the specimen in the second photo is, is another job for guessers. Coyotes do mate with dogs and the result is known as a coy-dog. Coyote, coy-dog or just plain dog, this fierce appearing animal was shot in Saratoga County, mounted, and displayed in an Amsterdam business establishment.

One of the most famous of all Adirondack "characters," (and the phrase is used affectionately) was the late Jacques Suzanne of Lake Placid. Suzanne came to this country from France, crossing Europe and Siberia by dog sled, then across the Bering Straits, into Canada and the United States. A friend of the author, he raised malemutes and timber wolves at his Bear Cub Road property at Lake Placid, and was often called upon by the movie industry to furnish trained animals. He is posed with a mounted wolf. Suzanne died at the Essex County Infirmary at Whallonsburg in 1967.

THE PANTHER

Panthers, or mountain lions, as described in a previous chapter (Bounty Hunter) once roamed the Adirondacks freely, but were shot out of existence as pests. Although supposedly extinct in the mountain area, occasional sightings are reported. This is a photo of one of two cubs raised by the author. It is approximately two months old, shows the aggressive spark of adulthood and probably for good reason – it was on a diet of horsemeat and cod liver oil! This cub, a male, and its sister, eventually went to the State game farm at Delmar and when about 50 or 60 pounds each, killed each other over food. Fight occurred when the male attempted to express his dominance for the first time by eating from the food tray first.

Mac enthroned. Mac at the time of this writing was a tamed panther, pet of the Howard MacDonald family of Lake George Village. While shown chained, on occasion he roamed freely in the MacDonald yard and was a close pal of Patsy, the blind, 13-year-old MacDonald dog. Mac was one of a litter of four born at Animal Land, south of Lake George Village, owned by Paul Lukaris. During his early days, the lion often rode with MacDonald, Deputy Mayor and Police Commissioner of Lake George.

THE LYNX AND BOBCAT

Among other members of the cat family found in the Adirondacks are the bobcat at right in this Seagears painting, and the Canada lynx, above. The lynx is believed extinct by many, but this can be questioned. One mark which distinguishes one from the other is the tail. The lynx tail tip is completely black; the bobcat has black markings on the tail top. The bobcat, common, is also known as the wildcat or bay lynx.

Portrait of male bobcat in Winter coat. Drawn from captive trapped in Delaware County. Markings are typical.

CLAYT SEAGEARS

Bobcat in action is dramatically portrayed in this painting by Walter J. Schoonmaker. The cats will go after not only birds but small animals; they are sometimes accused of seeking fawns as prey. They also have been known to feed upon house cats. In Winter the bobcat will often feed upon Winter killed deer. Note black tip on top of tail in painting; as pointed out, this is a distinguishing mark of the bobcat.

THE PORCUPINE

The porcupine, "woods pig" or "porky," is one of the most common animals in the State; is considered a destroyer of timber because of its bark eating habits, thus often girdling a tree. Despite its armament of quills, a natural enemy is the fisher, a member of the weasel family, which will hunt down and consume a porky. The quills seem to have little effect upon the fisher and undersides of hides seen by the author have often been criss-crossed with the spines. A meeting of the porcupine and fisher is pictured on the next page, a sketch by Bill Fowler, a Maine artist who served in the U.S. Air Force.

THE TIMBER RATTLESNAKE

Snakes do indeed exist in the Adirondacks, but fortunately all save one are nonpoisonous, and most are of the common garden variety. The timber rattler is highly localized, can be found on Tongue Mountain at Lake George, and in the South Bay region of Lake Champlain. Under the bounty system, which no longer exists, the rattlers were hunted by such individuals as the late Willie Clark, above, photographed on the slopes of Tongue Mt. Clark lived north of Bolton Landing, used to sell the skins and produce "snake oil," used to "cure" rheumatism.

The timber rattler, seen above, caught by Jack Pinto, Times-Union Photographer, is not an aggressive reptile insofar as humans are concerned, and it will dodge a confrontation. No deaths have been recorded from its bite within the past half century. It is a powerful swimmer. In size and strength, however, it hardly compares to the Western and Southern varieties.

At right: A four-foot six-inch rattler is held by the late G.H. Schiller of Altamont, well known sportsman and gunsmith. The reptile was shot on Tongue Mt., in what Mr. Schiller called Willie Clark's famous "Pine Tree Den" on the eastern slope of the Mountain, facing Lake George's Narrows.

Like other snakes, the timber rattler is capable of wide expansion of its mouth. The fangs, which inject venom, are pictured, extended; when not in use, they fold back into the mouth. Poison is stored in glands one on each side of the jaw. The timber rattler is smaller than the Western Diamondback, which can attain a length of seven feet.

A common garter snake in trouble is shown below. This non-poisonous reptile was in the process of swallowing a frog whole, when it was interrupted, possibly by a predator. Ordinarily prey is devoured head first. In this case, obviously, the snake is trying to get rid of its food, since the amphibian is reversed.

THE OTTER

The otter, like the mink and marten, is a member of the weasel family, can be tamed and is a voracious eater and sometimes senseless killer of fish. One now-closed State hatchery lost 1,000 salmon a day for five days before the animal's depredations were stopped. At right a curious beast appears through a hole of the kind cut by ice fishermen; on occasion, fishermen literally have hooked hungry otter on tipups, hauled them to the surface, thinking they had a new world's record fish! Otters will use such apertures as "breather holes" as they prowl beneath lake ice on forays for food.

Lower photo illustrates graceful lines of the animal as it rests on land. The otter is playful; "otter slides" often are seen in Winter. These are nothing more than chutes in snow, made as the animal slides downhill.

THE BEAVER

Beaver, to all practical purposes once extinct in the Adirondacks, are back in full force. A member of the rodent family, it is one of the most fascinating animals to study and watch. Photos in this section were taken by Walter J. Schoonmaker and the author. The beaver above approaches a sapling to partake of a meal of bark. This animal is capable not only of felling good sized trees, such as birch or poplar, but will strip them entirely.

The magnificent head shot of a beaver was snapped by Schoonmaker as it swam near a blind he had set up. Lower photo shows difficulties canoeists have in surmounting beaver dams. Jack Malone, formerly of Schenectady, and Ray Ellis of Burnt Hills, are shown bulling their craft over a dam on a feeder creek to Sacandaga Lake in Hamilton County. Some dams are so well constructed they are broken only by blasting.

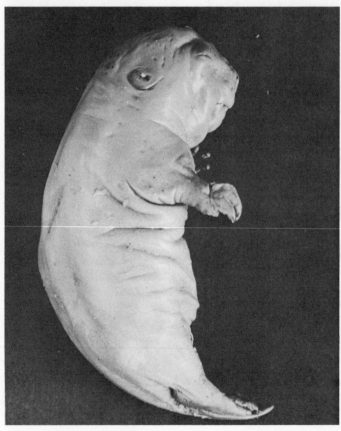

Top left: Birch on Oswegatchie River felled by beaver; roll of film shows comparative size. Top right: Two of the animals busy feeding on twigs and leaves, and lower left: Beaver stripping sapling. Fetus of beaver shown in other photo.

106

The beaver house is constructed of small and large cuts, chewed to size and interlaced with extraordinary skill. The house pictured is at the Pack Forest at Warrensburg. Lower photo shows beaver pond; when these natural engineers dam a stream, water backs up with no regard to tree or plant life. Some property owners view these reservoirs as nuisances. The North Country is covered with small ponds which would not exist today were it not for the beaver. So the "nuisance" question is open to argument.

THE BUFFALO

Historically a stranger to the North Country, the buffalo once did exist in New York State and some believe penetrated as far as Syracuse. During prehistoric times the bison probably existed throughout the hill country, or at least on its fringes. Today there are buffalo in the Adirondacks, a small herd at the Miner Center at Chazy, Clinton County. Under no circumstances can herd members be considered tame; they live both in a wooded area and in open fields.

When the photo above was snapped by the author, the buffalo at Miner Center were skittish and with good reason; a new born calf was being protected. Note how adults keep calf in center as group moves by photographer. Animal such as the bull at left may weigh 1,500 to 2,000 pounds. Temperamentally, they are totally unpredictable. Skulls such as this once dotted the western plains by the millions as the buffalo was shot deliberately out of existence not only to deprive Indian nations of food source, but to furnish such delicacies as buffalo tongue — and, of course, the famous buffalo robe.

THE BLACK CROWNED NIGHT HERON

Before the bird comes the egg. And out of the egg comes a young black crowned night heron, busily pecking its way into the Great Society. This bird is considered rare in the Adirondacks, but the High Peaks Audubon Society says it does breed on Four Brothers Island in Lake Champlain. The photos were taken in a herony or rookery in the Mohawk River.

Black crowned night herons will utilize one tree for several nests. In this photo of Nick Drahos inspecting one, four are visible; they are roughly made of small sticks and twigs. Death rate is high in a rookery; in some instances adults or growing young will strangle themselves in the crotch of a tree.

Top left: A young heron, able to climb and flap its way for short distances. Top right: A hungry youngster still in its nest. Two adult herons in lower photo are perched on floating log surrounded by water chestnut weed. The herons are fish eaters but have been observed eating small snakes, frogs, worms, snails and other small forms of life. Carp, shot during the Spring spawning season by the author with bow and arrow, were flung on the shore of the rookery and visits a few days later found the carcasses stripped clean. The heron is sometimes called the "Quawk," because of its cry.

112

THE EAGLE

The American, or bald eagle, is an endangered species not only in the Adirondacks, but throughout most of America because of widespread use of pesticides, which affect their eggs — and, of course, because of encroachment of humans upon their domains. Few, if any bald eagles are permanent residents of the Adirondacks; most of them sighted are migrants. Hopefully under the wilderness area zoning, these magnificent birds will return.

THE CHIMNEY SWIFT

An interesting phenomenon has occurred every May at Northville, a community on the shores of the Sacandaga Reservoir, now renamed the Great Sacandaga Lake. Chimney swifts, after spending Winters in the Amazon River basin in South America, return to the Hubbell Memorial, a chimney of an old factory, where they live the Summer through. This photo of their arrival and nose-dive into their home was made at 8:45 p.m. on May 6, a few years ago. They drop into the chimney as though poured from a coffee percolator.

THE MONK PARAKEET, NEW PEST

Newest pest-import in the North Country is the Monk Parakeet from South America; a crateful of these crop eating birds broke at Kennedy Airport and they have spread rapidly; eventually may pose a serious threat to fruit and other crops. Pictured is a youngster a few weeks old. Bottom shows size of sticks used in communal nests; as many as ten families may live in compartments in one nest, some bigger than a bushel basket. The parakeet possesses a harsh, squawking voice; is about 12 inches in length, green with yellowish belly and a gray breast and facial mask. In some areas in South America they have destroyed 45 percent of fruit and grain crops.

MR. FRAGRANT

Little is needed to be said about the skunk and its remarkable powers of making its presence known and respected. The animal can, however, be tamed. At left Mr. Fragrant walks the piano keyboard with an unusual backdrop, a song entitled "Unchained Melody." Lower photo shows a little fellow enduring a bath.

While this animal is known for its power of projecting its personality up to distances of ten feet, it ordinarily will not use artillery unless threatened. This has been a source of considerable solace for many.

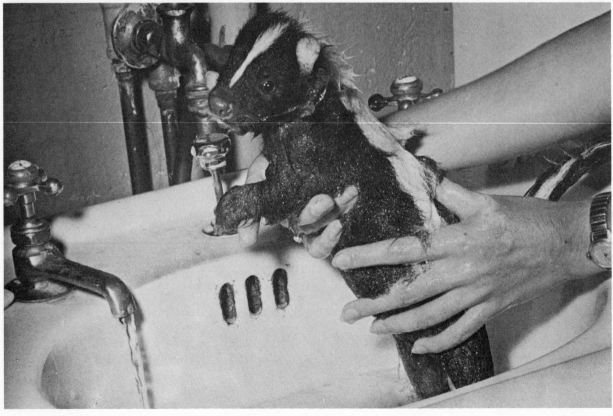

THE FISHER – AND A MOUSE HIJACK!

Shown in these sketches by Walter J. Schoonmaker are the fisher, a member of the weasel family, once thought extinct in the Adirondacks, but now returned, and a snowy owl in pursuit of a mouse which has little desire to be part of the big bird's evening meal. The snowy owl is a migrant; often confounds viewers by appearing in cities.

SMALL FRY

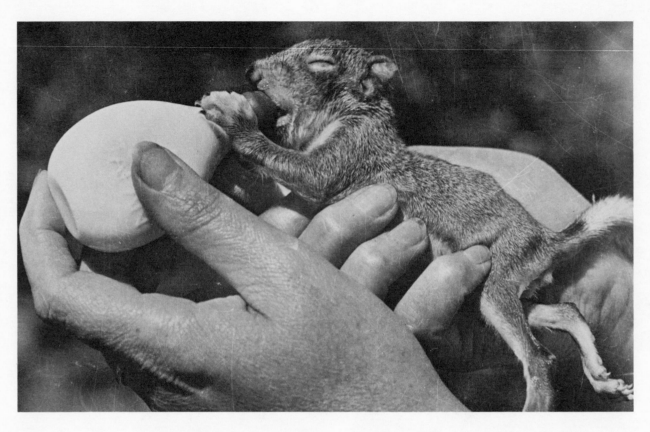

The gray squirrel is a common sight. Here's a new born feeding from a bottle of warm milk. It was orphaned by a hunter. Lower left: Young cottontail rabbit, common throughout the state, is cupped in hands after rescue from predator which killed its mother. Lower photo: Blitheful sprite and spirit is the common chipmunk, one of the true hibernators in the Adirondacks.

SMALL FRY

White footed field mouse, common and prolific, is a diet staple for many meat eaters, including snakes.

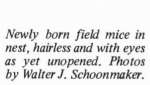

Newly born field mice in nest, hairless and with eyes as yet unopened. Photos by Walter J. Schoonmaker.

119

Twenty years ago the spruce forests of the Adirondacks constituted the last main stand of the marten, or American sable, pictured at upper left. Main enemies are their larger cousin, the fisher, and the great horned owl. The marten is so agile it can catch red squirrels with ease. Top right: Young foxes at opening of their den, located in the midst of a field. And in lower photo, the hairy tailed mole is pictured. Note powerful claws used in digging and wedge-shaped face, used to "push" its way through earth.

Young woodchucks, above, stand side by side, alert to possible danger. Once each was as small as the little fellow at top right; he's only three days old, with a skin like wet brown paper. Lower photo: A woodchuck can die from more than a hunter's bullet. This one succumbed to starvation because its teeth, instead of being worn to proper proportion, kept growing. Note top incisors and how they curled downward, inward and upward literally into the skull. These are Walter J. Schoonmaker photos.

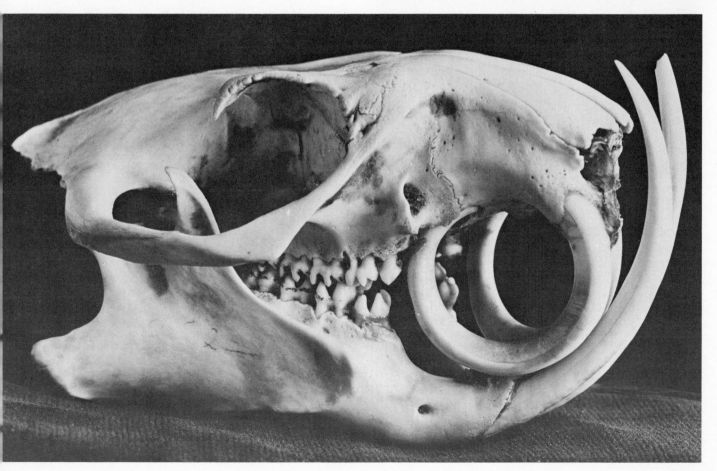

One of the tiniest of predators is the ant lion, an insect which digs, then quietly buries itself at the bottom of its hole. When an ant rolls down the incline, the powerful jaw of the "lion" closes upon it and doom is certain. These are ant lion pits, dug in the fine sand of a limestone area.

A ridiculous pose – "Frog on a Tack" – is what the wire services called it when it was published. The author found this tiny amphibian and hundreds of others in the Ticonderoga area and after expenditure of considerable patience got him to sit still on a thumb tack long enough for a photo! The picture will add nothing to the science of biology but does show comparative size.

SALMON "MILKING"

By gentle massaging, eggs from a landlocked salmon can be forced from the body of a female, into a shallow pan. The male salmon is then "milked" or stripped of its milt, or sperm, as shown above, and fertilization occurs instanteously in the pan. It is hardly a romantic method reproduction but the fish are unharmed and returned to the waters, and hatcheries have hundreds of thousands of eggs to process. This scene was taken at Lake George.

AND ANOTHER BIG ONE

This fish, netted by EnCon personnel during Fall, was caught along with the salmon on the preceding page. It is a brown trout. Netting operations were conducted at the southern end of Lake George and in addition to salmon and the brown trout, rainbows also were collected in the nets. The rainbows, however, spawn in Spring.

THE SNAPPING TURTLE

The author, while at Great Sacandaga Lake, formerly the Sacandaga Reservoir, once saw a snapping turtle of this size draw a duck underwater for a meal. This turtle had a shell approximately two feet long. The reptile, almost prehistoric in appearance, has tremendous strength in its jaws and is lightning fast as it strikes at waterfowl, or fish life. Snappers are found in streams and marshlands and, like other reptiles, are cold blooded.

The Pig Syndrome

This striking, though utterly useless and senseless example of "rock painting," greeted visitors who traveled the highway between Speculator and Indian Lake in Hamilton County. It is an example of despoilation in one of the most beautiful areas of the North Country and is a perfect example of The Pig Syndrome.

Litterbugging reflects a blighted attitude with a long and undistinguished background.

It is acne on the face of a Mona Lisa; warts on the nose of a John Barrymore, and carbuncles on the breast of Diane, virgin goddess of hunting.

The American, or bald eagle was once the dramatic emblem of America's might. The bird has since been replaced by the ubiquitous empty beer can, now the symbol of America's plight.

The first litterbug of any consequence in New York State was Henry Hudson, a British sea captain who did not discover but explored the river which now by no coincidence bears his name. His ship, the Half Moon, dumped its slops and junk overboard on its northward journey to Albany. Ships have been doing the same ever since. And now, of course, oil spills add to the river's misery.

In the 1700's the greatest litterbug was unquestionably the inept Gen. Abercrombie, another Britisher who, unsuccessful in his assault on French-held Fort Ticonderoga in 1758, ordered retreat. It was one done in such

desperation, haste and chaos that baggage, weapons and other accoutrements of the 16,000-man army were dumped not only along the shores of Lake George but into the lake itself.

The lake has been taking it on the chin ever since.

So has Lake Champlain. So have other bodies of well traveled waters in the Adirondacks.

Other sections of the North Country have not been ignored by the Assassins of Scenery who refuse to carry out what they carry in. Every year, for instance a special breed of such nature lovers see to it their mark is left in the Mt. Marcy region near Lake Placid.

A cleanup crew of Adirondack Mountain Club members in 1966 estimated at least five tons of garbage and other junk are left on the peak annually. At this rate, unless littering is stopped, Marcy will rise to new heights and climbers will tramp on a foundation of junk.

The rattle of tin and aluminum cans in many areas will replace the whisper of wind through the pines; the cry of the loon will be supplanted by the racket of bottles being smashed; the warning slap of the beaver

127

It can and does happen throughout the Adirondacks. Bears, attracted to town dumps, find tempting menus in such. But problems are created by unthinking onlookers, who consider the bears tame — when they are not. They are unpredictable and dangerous, should not be trifled with. Roy C. Higby of Big Moose Lake, in his book "A Man From the Past," said in one instance — a father tried placing his offspring on the back of a bear. . .for the ride!

tail on water will be superseded by the gurgle of oil cans, beer cans, soda cans and bottles as they sink beneath the waves, thus out of sight, out of mind.

All this is possible.

The famous King Philips Spring on the Keene Valley Road, just off the Adirondack Northway, widely known for years as a source of pure drinking water, and widely used by area residents to replenish their camp and cottage supplies, was closed in 1973 because of intolerable health conditions. Travelers had been using the locale as a public latrine and dumping ground.

Months later, after workers from the Department of Environmental Conservation cleaned and fenced the area the spring was reopened.

Balancing Rock, a magnificent, 25-ton boulder of anorthosite along Blue Ridge Road, is a spot where tourists often stop to use their cameras. This huge rock, 14 feet in diameter, was deposited by a glacier on its way to melt; it literally is balanced atop a rock outcropping.

While many travelers use the boulder as a backdrop for photos, others use it as a "canvas" upon which to

spray-paint initials and graffiti. Psychologists have long puzzled over this practice, but some have reached the conclusion it is a compulsive gesture on the part of the vandal to leave his sign. In different fashion dogs do the same on hydrants.

Still other travelers use the area behind the Balancing Rock as a garbage dump. The Pig Syndrome knows no special target. And it respects none.

During the Constitutional Convention in Albany in 1967 I traveled with a group of delegates and members of the Adirondack Mountain Club (sometimes referred to as the ADK) into the Murphy Lake area near Northville. The idea behind this hike was to give delegates a taste of Forest Preserve wilderness atmosphere. The leanto at the lake gave far more than that, however; it presented delegates with one of the finest garbage dumps in the preserve.

I have seen and remonstrated with fishermen throwing beer cans and lunch leavings into the clear waters of the Miami River in the Speculator area; I have seen picnic tables which had been smashed and thrown into the Jessup River, which feeds Indian Lake.

Prof. E.H. Ketchledge

Beer and soda cans sparkle under rays of the sun like eyes of wall-eyes under the beam of a flashlight as one paddles up the Oswegatchie River. I have seen the gleaming cans in the clear waters of the outlet to Brook Trout Lake, miles deep in the Forest Preserve.

Efforts of many organizations and agencies, including the Department of Environmental Conservation, the Adirondack Mountain Club, Sierra Club, local fish and game groups, and dozens of others, have warred ceaselessly against the mounting problem of litter, but the assault by the Tin Can Brigade has continued to grow.

One of these days Congress may change the National Emblem from the eagle to the six pack. One wonders why the New York State Legislature has not as yet made the can part of the State seal.

New York State's Department of Transportation has jurisdiction over some 14,000 miles of highway. The litter deposited on and along these highways costs three million dollars a year in manpower and equipment to clean up and dump properly.

Litter, said Commissioner Raymond T. Schuler, usually amounted to 15 cubic yards per mile along the 14,000 miles. And this, he said, "would rise to an unsightly pile three feet square and five stories high, if so arranged, along every mile of State highway!"

A nationwide survey sponsored by Keep America Beautiful and carried out by the Highway Research Board of the National Academy of Science, found an accumulation of one cubic yard of litter per mile a month as the national average. New York State, with a population per area well above most states, exceeded the average in the statistical sampling of the study.

Cleaning up the mess costs not only money but precious manpower — 650,000 man hours a year. And many of those hours are spent in the vastness of the Adirondack Park area.

Contained in this chapter are photos showing one of the bright spots in the litter picture. They represent efforts of the Adirondack Mountain Club to "scrub" Mt. Marcy. The formation of the cleanup crew was prompted by Prof. E.H. Ketchledge of Syracuse University, who found himself knee deep in junk when he climbed the peak. He wrote Theron C. Johnson of Schenectady, then president of the ADK. Johnson responded quickly; he had just appointed A.D. Coggeshall, also of Schenectady, as chairman of the organization's Clean Trailsides Committee.

A crew of 14 members of the ADK and Mohawk Valley Hiking Club was organized, climbed to Marcy's heights, there flattened cans, collected other junk, loaded it all into bags and carried it to Marcy Dam, from whence it was trucked to a landfill site in an EnCon vehicle. More than 400 pounds were thus carried along Marcy's trails, an astonishing amount, since crew members also carried other needed equipment.

Coggeshall, incidentally, is among outdoor leaders who have during the past several years been promoting ski-touring, or cross-country skiing. The hiking club mentioned was, in the 1930's, the organization mainly responsible for pinpointing North Creek as a major ski resort area.

Now grown to more than 9,000 members, the ADK continues its efforts to counteract the rising flood of junk in the Adirondacks. The pilot project has been voted, involving what the club calls "three ridge runners." These are individuals employed by the club and whose sole purpose is to be helpful to hikers and campers. Part of their job will be to attempt to educate those who defile scenery by littering. It is a notable effort, one to be followed with interest.

Hopefully the day will come when all who use the Adirondacks will realize that to despoil will destroy the very quality which attracts. Perhaps, however, outdoorsmen are fighting a losing battle. Perhaps the Pig Syndrome has reached out from the cities and has laid such hold upon the Hill Country that no amount of effort will counteract its insidious destructive tendencies.

If this ever happens, it will total tragedy. The Assassins of Scenery will have had their way.

This was the dismal scene in the haze of an Adirondack day at the Indian Falls leanto on the way to Mt. Marcy's peak. Such scenes are totally uncalled for anywhere, let alone in this beautiful section of the High Peak country. Yet "nature lovers," seeking beauty, assassinate it by not carrying out what they carry in. This photo and others of the Mt. Marcy cleanup were taken by A.D. Coggeshall of the Adirondack Mountain Club.

Ray Michalowski, Will Merritt, Clark Gittinger and Karl Schmieder, all of Schenectady, participating in Operation Can Flattener. Cans were crushed between hinged two-by-fours for easier carrying off Mt. Marcy.

Other methods of flattening were used. Here David Vermilyea, also Schenectady, used a rock to crush discarded containers. Note pile still to be processed.

Elwyn Bigelow and Clark Gittinger, Schenectady, load sacks with junk collected from Marcy, preparatory to the long journey downwards. Other photo: starting down the trail with pack boards loaded are Bigelow, Schmieder and James Spring. The entire cleanup crew carried more than 400 pounds off Marcy!

Skin divers, angered by littering off the shore of the Hearthstone public campsite, drew volunteers from the Albany, Troy and Schenectady areas for a massive cleanup. More than 13 trash cans of junk were collected. Participating personnel: Philip DeRing, Jack Marx, John Burns, John Rudt, Ray Velten, Doug Rodriguez, Joe Baldwin, Dan Kawola, Ted Cook, Ronald Hems, Norm Shapiro, Mike Peparella, Fred Riedell, Jim Magenis, Marchia Casey, D. Kagel, Dick Hayes, Rick Ketterer, Bob Frame, Dick Kildoyle, Dow Nye, Don Sutliff, Dave Priester, Barbara Hamil, Bill Guthinger, Lee Gould and Art Dickerson.

William Dow of the Lake George Steamboat Company, furnished the Mohican as a base of operations.

In the other photo, a Lake George Park Commission patrolman lifts a plastic bag of human feces, found floating in the lake. Littering of this lake in any form is illegal. Violators receive stiff penalties.

133

The author recorded the above scene during a canoe trip into Northwest Bay of Lake George. The locale is Montcalm Point, tip of Tongue Mountain. Careless picnickers or campers dumped this trash into the clear waters; included were broken bottles, beer cans, cartons and other throwaways. Second photo shows results of additional cleanup by skin divers off the shores of Long Island in the same lake. A continued educational program on littering is conducted not only by the Lake George Park Commission but the Lake George Association as well. Such scenes are by no means confined to this body of water.

After enjoying use of this picnic table along the Jessup River, picnickers smashed part of it, threw the remains into the stream. This is an area of the Jessup which also serves as a dumping ground for containers. Lower photo shows a roadside rest area at Lake Durant, on the way to Blue Mountain Lake. Total disregard for beauty, cleanliness and the rights of others is evidenced. This is not picnic trash; it is house garbage. State facilities at such roadside stops, as well as along the Northway are heavily — and illegally used for such purposes.

Melting snows along such scenic highways as the Adirondack Northway all too frequently disclose this type of discouraging sight. Here, scattered up and down the length of a rest area, is junk discarded by individuals who couldn't care less. Yet they would be the first to protest if their own yards were used in similar fashion. On the road through beautiful Keene Valley, picnickers with a twisted sense of humor, used this tree crotch as a garbage disposal.

For some reason some users of State leantos continually foul their own nest. Here is a garbage dump only a few feet from the Miami River leanto, on the trail into Pillsbury Lake.

This may be a sign of the times, but some refuse to pay attention. Because some find town landfill areas closed at certain hours, they dump their garbage outside the closed gate.

Devil Weed

**Ninety Years Ago The Water Chestnut Began
Its Throttling Activities. Now The Plant
Is Being Conquered.**

As a transplant from Europe, the water chestnut or Trapa natans has been received about as well as the monk parakeet, English sparrow, the starling, gypsy moth and the Dutch elm blight.

To fishermen, swimmers and boaters this plant is as welcome as a case of hives on a hot Summer's day. It is an annual which clogs, chokes and strangles the area in which it grows. It is as content in polluted waters as in pure.

Some say the chestnut was first placed in Collins Lake in Scotia, a community across the Mohawk River from Schenectady, because of the plant's "beauty." It bears small flowers. Others say it was put into the spring fed lake as a food source. For whom or what is not specified. Scotians seem well fed without it and the lake has never reported a monster.

If it is beautiful, beauty should be viewed from a distance; the weed prompts colorful language when the bare foot comes into contact with its seeds, pointed pods protected by barbed spines every bit as vicious in impact as porcupine quills.

Not strange is that it is also referred to as the Devil Weed.

As far as food is concerned, several hundred of the seed nuts were steamed in a Cornell University experiment some years ago and later served boiled or baked with tasty sauces to 60 individuals. Fifteen said they liked the taste — but they didn't ask for the recipe. The experiment died a natural death.

The plant reached Europe from Asia. Reportedly it is eaten in China but in China birds' nests are also considered delicacies. There is one indisputable point. In America the water chestnut will never replace the peanut. It will, as a matter of gastronomical fact, replace nothing. It is as unwanted as a cat about to give birth to a litter.

The Collins Lake planting reportedly occurred in 1884. Untold millions of descendants have grown from those first few. None seem to have died. From Collins Lake the plant floated down the outlet into the Mohawk River and from the Mohawk went into the Hudson where it grabbed hold as far south as far as Peekskill.

It also "floated" upstream into southern Lake Champlain's Narrows, presumably transported by barges up the Hudson to Fort Edward, then through Lock 7 of the Champlain Division of the Barge Canal. Barges eventually leave the canal at Whitehall and use Champlain to reach northern New York State and Vermont ports.

The weed's power of "floating" also enabled it to reach Dunham Bay, Lake George, an improbable but reported fact. Lake George has no water connection with Hudson's River.

It has also gone upstream in the Mohawk; has been noted in Round Lake and Saratoga Lake in Saratoga County. It even reached the Tomhannock Reservoir, Troy. In travels it is as astonishing as the walking catfish causing consternation in Florida.

Plight of the outboard owner is dramatized in photo taken during the 1930's along shoreline of Collins Lake. Progress through the weed bed was slow, often impossible because props became snarled in the long stems. On the following page upper photo shows the extent to which the water chestnut choked the lake. Lower photo, also taken in the 1930's, shows "navigable" portion of the Mohawk River in the so-called Niskayuna pool area.

Today the Department of Environmental Conservation seems to not only have stopped its spread but seems well on its way to eliminating the pest. The spraying program (the weed is "hit" twice annually) is aimed at some 6,700 acres; at one time was a holding operation, but not now, said Dr. Paul Neth, of EnCon's Bureau of Fish. The anti-weed program apparently is cutting the weed to midget proportions.

This writer first became aware of the "spreading chestnut" in the early 1930's, when it had all but throttled Collins Lake and was sending massive feelers into the Mohawk. Efforts made to eliminate it in those early days were manual — and not too successful.

Photos in this chapter will give the reader some idea of the choking power of the pest.

The plant became such a nuisance that in 1949 the State declared it illegal to plant, transport, transplant or even traffic in the water chestnut, or the seeds or nuts thereof. The law also specifically prohibits encouraging the growth of the plant.

Seeds are capable of producing stems from six inches to 15 feet long! Each supports one or more rosettes of leaves which float on the surface, buoyed by a bladder-like growth in stems of the outer leaves. The rosettes appear during May or early June and die in Autumn. Small white flowers appear during July and each flower is capable of developing into the floral version of the porcupine.

Comments EnCon officials:

"In areas where this plant is established, fishing, boating and swimming are impossible. Water flow is impeded which promotes silting, stagnation and the breeding of mosquitoes. At the same time valuable food plants for waterfowl and other wildlife are crowded or prevented from becoming established.

"Large quantities of the barbed nut-like seeds are also produced annually which tend to wash up on beaches. Stepping or sitting upon these barbed nuts usually results in a very painful wound."

All of which is true. Ask anyone who has sat on one.

Tenacity evidenced by the water chestnut in seeking new habitats and clinging to them is apparent in this photo taken along the western shore of the Hudson River near Mechanicville. Seeds for this growth were transported inadvertently by barges, since the Mohawk, carrier of the plant pest, empties into the Hudson far downstream. And the seeds, as yet anyway, haven't learned to swim against a current.

The Grandmother Tree

Professor Shelley W. Potter, Jr., Pack Forest Manager, explains history of The Grandmother's Tree to Timothy L. Barnett, Executive Director, Adirondack Conservancy Committee, as the Potter family pet, Brandy, lends an attentive ear (or two). The giant tree exists on one of the comparatively few virgin tracts in the Adirondacks and will live out its life untouched by chain saw or axe.

Of the astronomical number of trees in New York State comparatively few have dramatic stories to tell.

The Grandmother's Tree at the Charles Lathrop Pack Forest north of Warrensburg, off Route 9, is one of them.

This patient giant was 81 years old when the French and Indian War swirled viciously throughout the Eastern Adirondacks in 1755.

It was 102 years old when the Declaration of Independence was signed in 1776.

It had reached the ripe old age of 138 when the War of 1812 burst upon the North Country in all its naval fury on Lake Champlain.

Today the huge white pine, now entering its third century, stands 165 feet tall, is four-feet, four-inches in diameter at chest height (about five feet) and holds more than 4,000 board feet of lumber, enough to build a small, one story home. Its stump value is about $400. Its worth to history and modern man is incalculable.

The old Adirondack patriarch is healthy; its crown towers over other growth in the 47 acres of virginal forest at the Pack Forest, set aside a score of years ago as a "natural area in perpetuity," an area where no man had created a disturbance by axe or saw. If fire touched upon the scene, it left no mark. These 47 acres rest within the six square miles of the Pack Forest, which is a field campus for the State College of Environmental Sciences and Forestry at Syracuse.

The wooded campus has nature trails and is visited by thousands annually.

The tree is of such massive weight that its base literally has developed the familiar folds of the circus fat lady. These can be seen in the accompanying photograph. If it has seen history, has heard thunder and escaped the ravages of lightning, it will have years to see and hear even more. Professor Shelley W. Potter, Jr., Pack Forest Manager, says it will never be touched by chain saw or axe. When it dies, it will die a natural death, crashing to the forest floor, opening a huge swath, thus in death offering open space to struggling new growths. Such is the cycle in a natural forest.

How this virginal tree survived the age of ruthless lumbering makes the story. It starts back in 1796 when the Woodward family moved into the Warrensburg area; the family's early home now serves as a guest house on Pack Forest lands. The lumberman's axe indeed touched upon the immediate area between 1830 and 1840 but the acres upon which The Grandmother's Tree now stands were inaccessible because of intervening swamps. Lumbermen, interested only on skimming the evergreen cream, by-passed the boglands.

In 1870 the story continues to unfold. Mrs. Margaret Woodward's husband had promised her a set of pewter ware. Financially the times were harsh; depression stalked the region. He decided to raise money by felling the tree; by this time the swampland had dried because the course of the stream which fed it had changed.

But Mrs. Woodward put her foot down hard. The tree, she said, was not be cut. She could do without her gift. Her husband gave in. Presumably he went to other trees. But the Big Tree stood firm and tall and from that day on it became known by its present title.

Today it continues to periodically produce its cones, seeds for future generations. It watches bear, otter, beaver, deer, fisher, fox and many other animals prowl its base.

Equally imperturbably it watches time flow on.

The individual who saved it is long gone.

The Grandmother's Tree is a monument to the woman who decided that continued life was more important than a set of metal utensils.

Frontier Forts

**As Armies Moved and Won They Left Their
Sign Behind in a String of Fortifications,
Some of Which Have Been Reconstructed**

An astonishing bit of fireside conjecture would be that one World War Two machine gun with its ability to spit instant death by the score could have won a continent for England or France in the mid-1700's when weapons were primitive in construction, range, accuracy and power of devastation.

Pursuing imagination further, one similar weapon could have been the scythe of death that might have saved America during the Battle of Bunker Hill.

But this is pure conjecture.

When armies began marching in the mid-eighteenth century they depended upon the far less sophisticated weapons of the day, the musket, cannon, bayonet, knife, hatchet or the sword. And as armies marched and won they had to consolidate their bases.

Thus came into being the line of forts on the "Warpath of Nations," the navigable waterways of the Hudson River, Lake George and Lake Champlain.

Fort Edward, "the carrying place," came into existence in 1755 on the Hudson, downstream from Glens Falls. Here armies moving upstream on the Hudson disembarked because of rapids. To the north in the same year Sir William Johnson built Fort William Henry at the head of Lake George. In the same year the industrious French began construction of Fort Ticonderoga, then called Carillon, at Ticonderoga on Lake Champlain.

Northward was Fort St. Frederic, built in 1730 by the French at Crown Point. Nearby Fort Amherst came into existence in 1759.

During the Revolution, Mt. Defiance, which over looks Fort Ticonderoga, was armed by the British in 1777. This 856-foot peak, now owned by the Historic Mt. Defiance Corporation, headed by James M Lonergan, is believed to be the first mountain in the United States to have a road built to its summit. Visible from Mt. Defiance is the blockhouse at Fort Mt. Hope an outpost of Fort Ticonderoga constructed originally in 1776 and strengthened in 1777. It was at Fort Mt Hope that Gen. Burgoyne's engineers conceived the idea of building the highway up Mt. Defiance to assure the British of firepower supremacy over Fort Ticonderoga then held by American forces.

Fort Mt. Hope is controlled by Carroll Lonergan and like Mt. Defiance, is open to the public.

Fort William Henry is reconstructed today. So is For Ticonderoga. Fort St. Frederic is in ruins. So is For Amherst, part of the Crown Point Reservation. For Edward has vanished; it was merely a mound of earth in the early 1800's.

Other forts were constructed during the two war mentioned but were minor and little or no trace of them exists today in the southeastern Adirondacks.

As an introduction to this chapter, let us take the discovery of the oldest unexploded mortar shell found on the North American continent in October, 1954. The story begins on the next page.

144

Fort William Henry, strongest outpost between Albany and Ticonderoga, was razed and its garrison massacred in August, 1757 by Montcalm's French and Indians. During the siege a mortar shell was lobbed into the fort from a point approximately where the Lake George High School now stands. Sketch by Charles Hawley illustrates method of firing the shell.

It landed in the ruins of a barracks building of the type pictured – the building has been reconstructed.

It did not explode. It glanced off the head of a defender, tearing off part of his scalp, and, landing upside down, its fuse was extinguished.

In October, 1954, two centuries after the shell was fired, it was found by staff archeologist Ernest Clute. Photo shows exact position. Astonishingly, atop the shell, was a tomahawk blade.

Even more startling was that when the seal of resin and tar was broken (shown in second photo) black human hair was found embedded in the material. A sample sent to the New York State Police Laboratory was analyzed and a report from then Director William Kirwan indicated it was "black hair from a human head, highly brittle," and of considerable age.

The heavy shell indeed had literally scalped a fort defender!

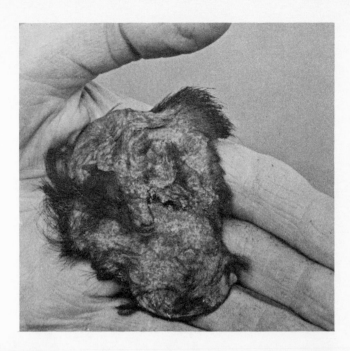

A demolition squad from Fort Jay, under Capt. Robert E. Swarthout of the 542d Ordnance Detachment, Explosive Ordnance Disposal Control, deactivated the shell, filled with black powder, damp near the metal but dry in the center. A closeup of the seal, with human hair attached, is shown.

The emptied shell is now on display at the fort museum. There is little question but that it is the oldest unexploded mortar projectile ever found on the continent.

When Fort William Henry was being rebuilt archeologists found prehistoric stone artifacts. Staff archeologist Stanley Gifford inspects a cache of roughed-out flints found in the fort's inner courtyard. Insert is a sandstone axe, believed to have come from Pennsylvania as a trade item during early Indian days when the area was used as a hunting and fishing site.

148

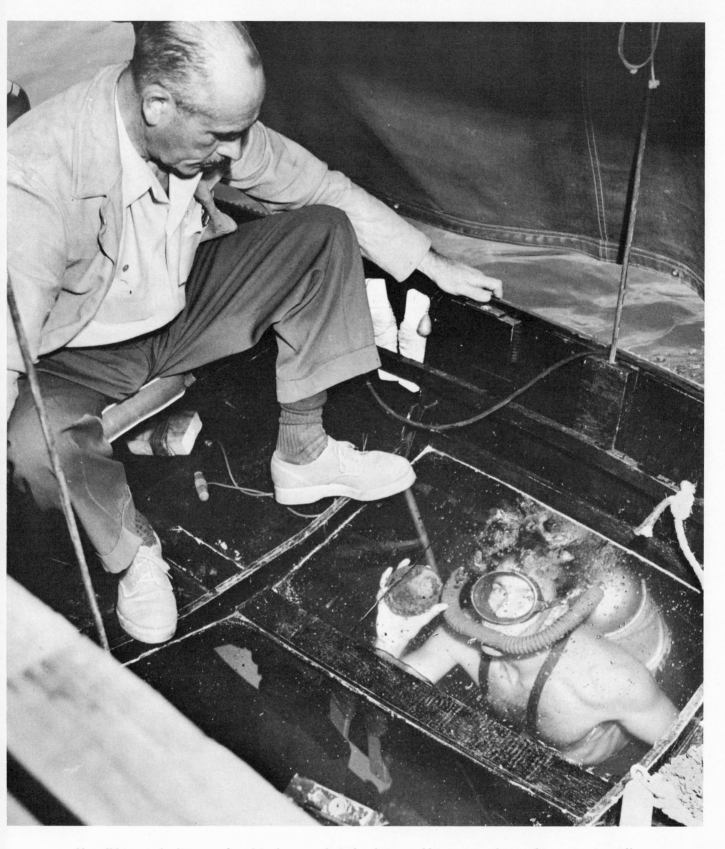

Not all historical relics were found in the ground. A glass bottomed boat was used to explore waters just off the fort. Here, watched by Harold G. Veeder, a diver rises to the glass panel holding a cannon ball found in the mud of the lake's bottom.

On the following page the diver rises with a three pronged French anchor. Lower photo, same page, shows uncovering of victims of the massacre, patients in the fort's hospital, killed and scalped by Montcalm's Indian allies. Many were afflicted with smallpox and the Indians carried the disease back to Canada. Note broken skulls, caused by tomahawk blows. Also note charred timbers at top of photo.

During routine excavations near the vicinity of the fort buried British or American warriors of the past were often found. Here Dr. Carl Guthe, State Archeologist at the time of the fort's reconstruction, inspects partially uncovered remains of a garrison member. While many died from wounds, many also died from disease.

Another archeologist, working in a trench sunk during early reconstruction days, holds the skull of a fort defender. Most of the burials occurred without coffins; some were laid to rest wrapped in a blanket, but such items were scarce and many were buried without covering. Depth ranged from five to six feet.

In one section of the grounds outside the fort this portion of a mass graveyard was uncovered. Individual burial sites were carefully staked out and archeologists probed the mounds with great care. Many of the victims, as previously pointed out, died with musket balls still within their bodies. Medical care was not of the best in those violent days.

Created especially for this volume, this painting shows a member of Rogers Rangers, with a portion of Fort William Henry in the left background. The painting is by Gary Zaboly of 3935 Blackstone Avenue, New York City, a young artist who has made an intensive study of the Rangers and who is considered an authority on the famous corps. He has authored and published several historical articles ranging from the French and Indian War to the Mexican War.

This painting displays a Ranger of 1756 in Summer campaign and hunting attire, the frock of which is based upon an actual deerskin shirt now in the Fort Ticonderoga museum. Says the artist:

"He wears the common bearskin cap, worn before the Scotch bonnet became the Rangers' official headgear, as well as the belt axe or tomahawk, musket and powderhorn."

At times — and there were many — the garrison at Fort William Henry was not the best equipped. Winters were harsh; disease and wounds kept many hospitalized. It should be remembered the fort was literally a frontier outpost and transportation of supplies from Albany was difficult and dangerous. The figure depicted above was created to illustrate one phase of life at the fort. Living was not easy with the French and Indian allies ever on the prowl.

155

The 1757 massacre has been portrayed in many ways. On this and the following page are two versions. Above is a famous painting by J.L.G. Ferris, used courtesy of The Glens Falls Insurance Company, a member of the Continental Insurance Companies. It shows the desperate attempt by Gen. Montcalm to stop his Indian allies from attacking departing garrison members after the fort's surrender. Montcalm's efforts did not succeed and the butchery of the helpless, unarmed column of men, women and children by drink-maddened Indians began.

On the following page is an old print depicting the same assault.

This excellent aerial view of Fort Ticonderoga, taken by Glens Falls photographer Richard K. Dean, shows the outstanding military position occupied by the "great stone fortress." The scene is facing south, with Lake Champlain in the background. While the Pell family began rebuilding Ticonderoga in 1830, there are portions of the fort still under reconstruction, so great is the care used in revitalizing the past. The fort's collection of cannon is considered the best in the United States.

After the massacre at Fort William Henry an English army of 16,000 under the inept Gen. Abercrombie gathered at the fort's ruins in 1758 for a revenge assault against Ticonderoga. The army sailed in more than 1,000 boats and rafts, landed, and promptly met with disaster. Lord Howe, considered the real British leader, fell in the first encounter with the French. Delay on the part of Abercrombie completed the catastrophe. In one charge more than 2,000 troops died. Panic stricken, Abercrombie retreated down Lake George, abandoning baggage and supplies not only on land but in the lake itself.

The painting of the embarkation of the expedition by F.C. Yohn is used courtesy of The Glens Falls Insurance Company.

There is an interesting legend behind this painting of the attack on Fort Ticonderoga by the "Am Freiceadan Dubh," or the famous Black Watch regiment during the Abercrombie expedition. The High-landers lost 647 killed or wounded in a little more than three hours, trying to penetrate an abatis of trees with sharpened branches cut by the French.

Among those wounded was Major Duncan Campbell of Inversaw, Scotland, age 55, who died nine days after the July 8 attack. Legend has it Campbell years before had unknowingly offered shelter and protection at his Scottish castle to a murderer who proved to be the slayer of Campbell's cousin, Donald.

The ghost of the victim appeared three times at Inversaw and on the third visit warned Campbell:

"Farewell Inversaw; farewell till we meet at Ticonderoga!"

Campbell at that time had never heard of Ticonderoga. But he was with the Black Watch and his fate was sealed.

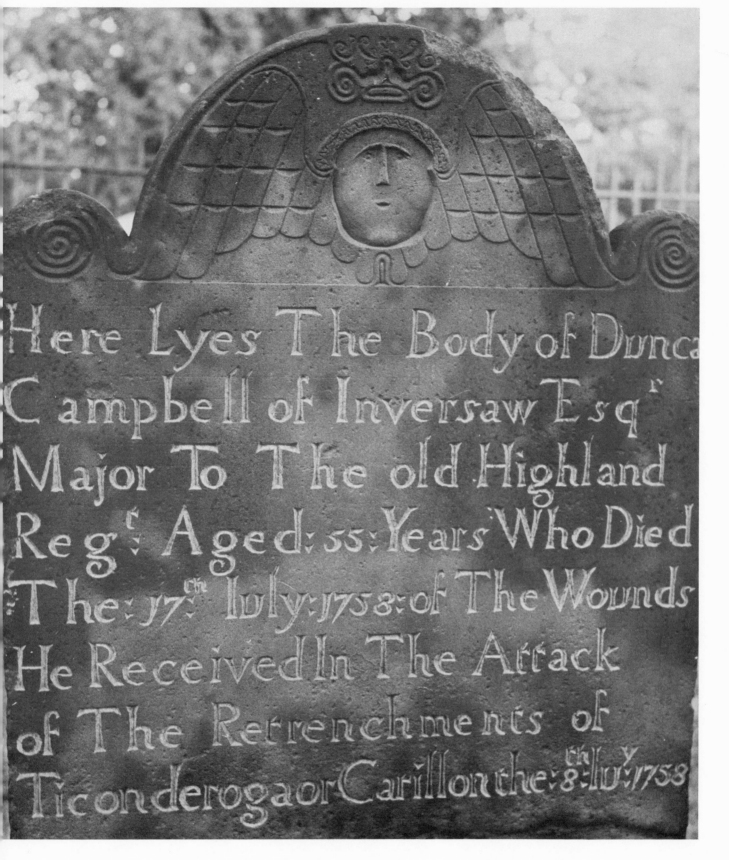

Major Campbell died of arm wounds at the military hospital at Fort Edward. His body is buried in Union Cemetery between that community and Hudson Falls. Shown is his tombstone, with this inscription:

"Here Lyes the Body of Duncan Campbell of Inversaw Esq., Major to the Old Highland Reg't, Aged 55 Years Who Died the 17th of July, 1758 of The Wounds He Received in The Attack of the Retrenchments of Ticonderoga or Carillon the 8th July, 1758."

Fort Ticonderoga's collection of cannon is world famous. Arrow points to one in particular. Ornamental handles are shaped in form of lizards, shown above. Closeup of the crest, part of the bronze weapon, shows a simple bar. This denotes the "bar sinister," or "sinistre," the sign of illegitimate birth within the family whose crest adorns the cannon.

On the following page: Photo of cannon is self explanatory. Other shows grape shot and musket balls found 18 inches below ground surface on fort property. They were located among charred remains of a fire.

162

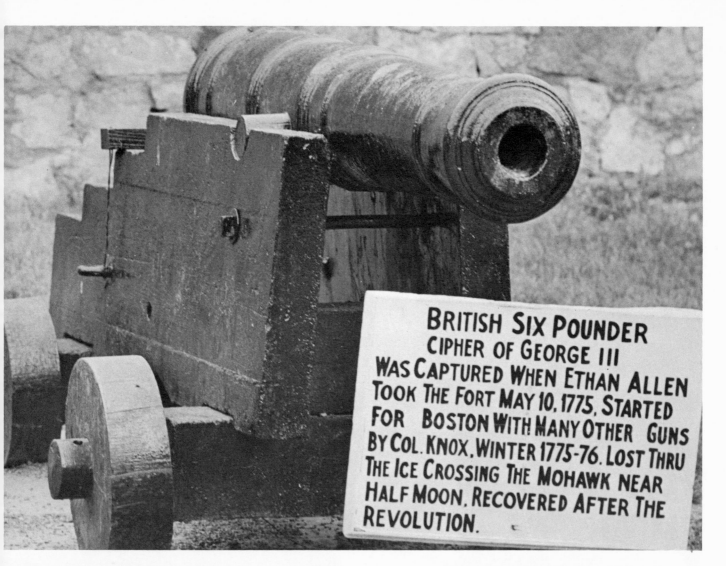

BRITISH SIX POUNDER
CIPHER OF GEORGE III
WAS CAPTURED WHEN ETHAN ALLEN
TOOK THE FORT MAY 10, 1775, STARTED
FOR BOSTON WITH MANY OTHER GUNS
BY COL. KNOX, WINTER 1775-76, LOST THRU
THE ICE CROSSING THE MOHAWK NEAR
HALF MOON, RECOVERED AFTER THE
REVOLUTION.

The military advantage of Mt. Defiance, topped with artillery by the British during the Revolution, can easily be ascertained. Lake Champlain stretches southward in this photo and Fort Ticonderoga (not pictured) is to the left. The modern highway, built by Historic Mt. Defiance, Inc., can be seen snaking its way to the summit from which point British cannon once dominated Ticonderoga, then occupied by American forces. The fort was evacuated.

— Winter Patrol —

CHRISTMAS AT FORT EDWARD · 1758

GARY ZABOLY
1973

Another painting by Gary Zaboly, this one showing a band of Rogers Rangers on early dawn patrol in the Fort Edward area during the Christmas of 1758. The painting is doubly interesting because it shows the relationship of buildings in the Fort Edward complex. Nearest building is the Royal Blockhouse.

Center background shows the main fortifications. The Rangers' headquarters are shown on the island and at far distant right is a second blockhouse on the west bank of the Hudson River. Time has seen the total disappearance of the entire complex, although Rogers Island has been under archeological excavation for several years.

Somber ruins of Fort Amherst on the Crown Point Reservation, Lake Champlain, are all that remain of a major military installation. Nearby are the ruins of Fort St. Frederic. These barracks buildings are open to the public but offer little except to those with vivid imaginations.

Like modern visitors the old-timers who prowled the Fort Amherst ruins were unable to resist leaving their sign behind. In these illustrated instances, names and dates have been chiseled into bedrock. Photo at lower left shows imprint of one F. Kirkbride, who visited the area in 1872 and spent time in carving not only his name and date but a pointing hand. The significance has been lost in time.

Thumbs Up on Pollution

The writer, present at a test of the Goggi device, known as Kleen-X-Zaust, snapped this photo of Charles Goggi at Tupper Lake. The measuring cup, almost full, represents discharge of raw gas and oil from a 75-horsepower motor over a period of approximately ten minutes.

A paradox in the fight for clean waters in New York State is that while voters over the past few years have approved bond issues of billions to cleanse their waterways, lakes and streams, the State itself, through a strange, sometimes unfathomable combination of circumstances, missed the boat years ago to stop pollution by outboard engines.

Do outboards pollute? Any owner or passenger in a boat powered by such an engine has seen and smelled the oil slick left in the wake of the craft.

It is estimated that despite new motors, which manufacturers claim do not discharge raw oil and gasoline, that at least five million gallons of such a mixture is spewed into the waters of the State every year b motors two years or older.

Lakes heavily used by outboards are in the positio of a prizefighter collapsing under a steady barrage c blows by his opponent while the referee stands idly b cleaning his fingernails.

The referee has, at times, been the New York Stat Legislature and at other times, the governor.

The tragic aspect is that pollution of this type cou have been stopped years ago. At least four times th Assembly passed a bill introduced by Assemblyma Glenn Harris of Fulton County mandating the use of simple, inexpensive device which not only prevents di charge but recycles fuel, a commodity more precious today than ever before. The bill has been killed by the Senate twice. When it did pass both houses, former Gov. Nelson A. Rockefeller, who proudly points to his efforts to clean State waters, vetoed it.

Major opposition to the device came, of course, from the outboard lobby, which claimed it would cost some 380,000 boat motor owners $35 million to install it. The lobby's mathematics is off base; the recycling device sold in 1974 for $34.95. A drain kit, which catches fuel which otherwise would be discharged, but does not recycle it, cost $12.

Charles Goggi, who invented the unit while at Lake George several years ago, sells it in cooperation with his brother, Eugene. Either unit is available from stock from Goggi International Ltd., 240 Main St., Danbury, Conn., 06810. So is literature.

Ronald Stewart of the Atmospheric Sciences and Research Center, State University of New York, and H.H. Howard, Department of Biology, Skidmore College, Saratoga Springs, in an article in the New York State Conservationist magazine, estimated a minimum of 40,000 gallons of fuel being discharged into lower Lake George each season. This was in 1968, and the lake area was from the village northward some ten miles to Tongue Mountain. One can imagine the growth of discharge since that time not only in Lake George, but other waters.

Conservative estimates involving motors two or more years old say ten percent of the fuel an owner pours into his tank goes into the water in raw state, unused. As oxygen content of any lake diminishes, the discharge becomes a contaminating factor and the ability to biologically degrade it is reduced. Contaminants thus remain, and pollutants levels rise until smell and taste of gasoline and oil will be noticeable in fish and water supplies.

What does this mean nationwide? A survey by the Federal Water Quality Administration in 1970 estimated that of approximately one billion gallons of outboard motor fuel sold annually, approximately 100 to 200 million gallons are dumped into State and Federal waters raw!

That's something to think about in view of today's gas and oil market.

Eugene Goggi is shown demonstrating use of the Goggi device at a meeting of the Adirondack Conservation Council, at Lake George. He holds tube connected to motor, which is discharging unburned fuel. The writer witnessed this test as well as several others, including one made at the annual convention of the New York State Conservation Council in Rochester.

Attractions and Memorabilia on Film

One of many great scenic attractions in the Adirondacks is High Falls Gorge, through which the famous Ausable River drops more than 100 feet. Railed walks and bridges furnish vantage points from which the turbulent rapids may be enjoyed. High Falls Gorge is at Wilmington, the community at which the Whiteface Mountain Memorial Highway begins.

Famous throughout the country is Storytown, U.S.A., located on Route 9, south of Lake George Village. This multi-million dollar development has been termed a literal fantasyland, featuring areas of fairy tale interest, a Ghost Town, Jungle Land and Alice in Wonderland sections. Below is a view of Enchanted Forest, located at Old Forge, showing the giant Paul Bunyan who greets visitors. Sound and animation add realism to visits with other storybook characters.

Many who visit the Adirondacks include a trip on the Lake Champlain Scenic Line Ferries, which cross to points in Vermont. The ride is a leisurely one of great beauty and convenience. Ferries leave from Port Kent, Essex and Grand Isle at frequent intervals. Below is a scene at Gaslight Village, Lake George, literally a throwback to the "Gay Nineties." Among its features: Silent movies, rides, and old fashioned "meller dramas."

The gustiness and action of the Old West is transferred to the Adirondacks at Frontier Town, located on Route 9 at North Hudson. It is also accessible from the Adirondack Northway, Exit 29. For a change of pace, many will also visit Santa's Workshop at North Pole, N.Y., located on the Whiteface Mountain Memorial Highway which begins at Wilmington. Those who wish may then continue seven miles to the summit of Whiteface Mountain; the highway is operated by New York State.

173

Land of Makebelieve at Upper Jay, is unusual in that it is built literally for children; the coach you see is miniature; the castle in the background is miniature. Its many activities and displays will delight child and adult alike. Visitors by the millions have seen what the Adirondacks have to offer. Among them were Russia's ambassador, Maxim Litvinov and Madame Litvinov, pictured at the Home of 1000 Animals, Lake Placid. The attraction features animal shows as well as exhibits of rare and valuable fur and game animals.

Considered the "Grand Canyon" of the East, Ausable Chasm is a truly magnificent and scenic area, located on Route 9, and accessible from the Adirondack Northway over Exits 34 or 35. A trip through the chasm is climaxed by a boat ride. The attraction is now in its second century of existence as a visiting area for tourists. (Photos of attractions listed, with exception of Ambassador and Madame Litvinov, by NYS Department of Commerce).

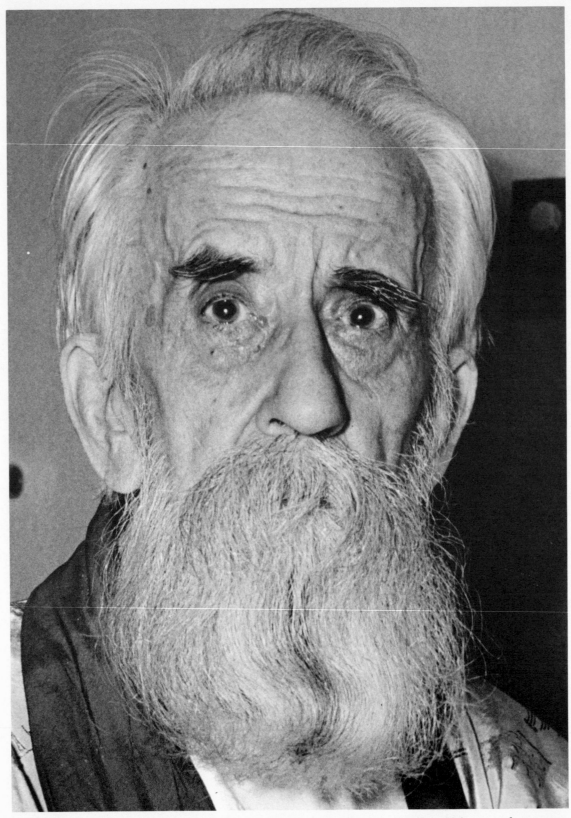

Noah John Rondeau, Hermit of Cold River, during his more than three decades of life as a recluse, was an attraction in his own way; his isolated cabin over years attracted thousands of hiking visitors. But age took over and Noah, a friend of the author's, was placed in Wilmington as a ward of Essex County. It was then I got to know him well. Taken to Placid Memorial Hospital in early August, 1967, the old gentleman weakened steadily and died August 24. You are looking at the last photo made of the famous Adirondack character; it was snapped only a few days prior to his death. What remains of Noah's past is at the Adirondack Museum at Blue Mountain Lake.

Above: Rondeau's cabin at the Adirondack Museum. Lower right: Rondeau in "city" clothes as he lived in his Wilmington home. This was the beginning of the sad years for the old gentleman. An insight into his earlier ones can be obtained from the photo, lower left, showing Rondeau, at right, with unidentified visitor. Photo taken by A.T. Shorey.

An excellent biography of Rondeau is "Noah John Rondeau, Adirondack Hermit," by Maitland C. DeSormo, Saranac Lake.

Rondeau's cabin is only one of a tremendous variety of exhibits at the Adirondack Museum. Here are others. Top: Steam engine once used on the Marion River Carry, shortest standard guage railroad in the world, used to portage steamboat passengers on the Marion River. Lower left: Snow roller used to pack down snow before the plow came into use. Lower right: Adirondack stagecoach.

The sign as one approaches reads: "Welcome. This is the historic village of Adirondack, settled in 1883." Owner is National Lead Industries, which mines titanium nearby. Thus the traveler has a chance to look at a North Country ghost town, once a busy mining community. Along the road is this MacIntyre Iron Co. blast furnace, first fired August 20, 1854. Iron was first mined, but processing ore became difficult because of an "impurity." The "impurity" turned out to be titanium of far greater economic value. Trails to Mt. Marcy start at northern end of the town. The area is known at Tahawus; is accessible from Route 28N between Minerva and Newcomb. Another route is the Blue Ridge Road, reachable from Northway Exit 29.

If one wishes to visit Tahawus via the Blue Ridge Road, one sight to see is the famous "Balancing Rock," 25 tons of Marcy anorthosite, 14 feet in diameter. This huge boulder, on the north side of the road, was left on bare bedrock by the retreating glacier and all too frequently has been misused by passersby. (See Page 128, "The Pig Syndrome.")

All boulders from the Marcy region were not glacially deposited in the Adirondacks. In second photo is one left by the ice mass on what is now Waverly Place, Schenectady. This rock, found by the late J.S. Apperson, later held a bronze plaque on Erie Boulevard, Schenectady, near the General Electric Company, until a new highway system rolled it into oblivion.

Some men when they die leave a monument for society to enjoy. J.S. Apperson of Schenectady, an aggressive fighter for the preservation of Lake George's beauty, wilderness character and cleanliness, was one of those men. His monument is Dome Island in Lake George, pictured above through an approaching rain mist. This island, purchased by Apperson many years ago to prevent commercial development of its 14 acres, was given to the Nature Conservancy and is perpetuated as wild land. When given in 1961, its appraised value was about $150,000. Apperson died at 84, Feb. 1, 1963 and is considered a giant in conservation circles. He is shown in typical pose in adjoining snapshot.

As mentioned, contrasts are numerous in New York State's North Country. For instance, here are two opposing forms of sculpture. Top one is located at the Northway (southbound lane) stop at Schroon Lake, and is titled "The Wheel." Some agnostics have termed it the "Adirondack Hernia." It reportedly cost New York State $5,000.

In Fulton County, however, there is the statue of Nick Stoner, noted Adirondack frontiersman, subject of a book by Donald R. Williams of Gloversville. The sculpture is located at Caroga Lake. So the battle between interpretive and realistic art continues, even in the Adirondacks where, actually, the realism of the mountains should be reflected in whatever statuary is erected.

182

Remarkable glimpses of the past come to light in hotel registers. Proof is in this entry in the guest book of the Trout Pavilion at Lake George, oldest hotel on the lake. It was made Sept. 11, 1877 and shows the arrival of Brigham Young of Salt Lake City and his wives. The noted Mormon leader brought nine with him, and there they are, Mrs. Brigham Young, 1st, Mrs. Brigham Young, 2nd, Mrs. Brigham Young, 3rd, etc. Interesting is that Young left his fortune of $3.5 million to his 21 wives, 55 children and one adopted child. He set up trust funds for each wife and her children. Seventy-seven people were involved, and not a single one of them attempted to break the will!

In the days when Brigham Young and his nine wives visited Trout Pavilion on Lake George's eastern shore, the only method of convenient travel was by boat. Steamboats plied the lake with regularity, carrying passengers, freight and mail; their arrivals were eagerly awaited. Today the lake has only one passenger steamboat in operation, the Minne-Ha-Ha, named after a former vessel, and operated by the Lake George Steamboat Company as an excursion craft. The Minne-Ha-Ha is driven by a stern paddle wheel and, with the Mohican and Ticonderoga, is a familiar sight. In the photo above, photographer unknown, she is passed by an electrically powered boat. Smaller steamboats, individually owned, are now growing more common — but are not numerous by any means.

When the author visited Skene Manor at Whitehall some years back for a talk before the Historical Society of that village, this was the remarkable sight he saw in a corner behind the bar of the restaurant. As an eye-catcher, the feminine hand protruding from a rocky crypt provoked questions. The answer was simple. The artificial hand, in essence, perpetuated a legend dating to the Revolutionary War. Major Philip Skene settled Whitehall in 1761, and it was then known as Skenesborough. He was a royalist and in 1775 his house was captured by American forces. In the cellar soldiers found the body of his wife, which had been preserved many years to secure to the husband an annuity devised to her "while she remained above ground!" The Americans reportedly buried the body in the rear of the house. So much for economic customs of the "old days!"

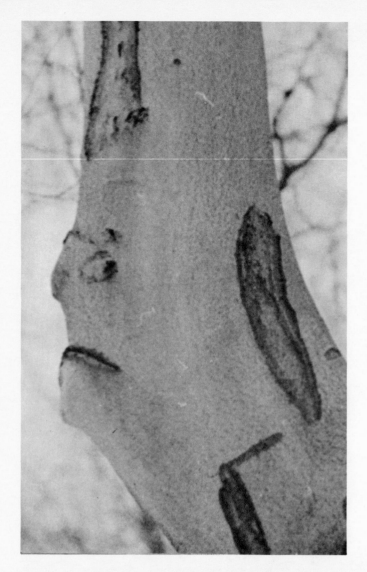

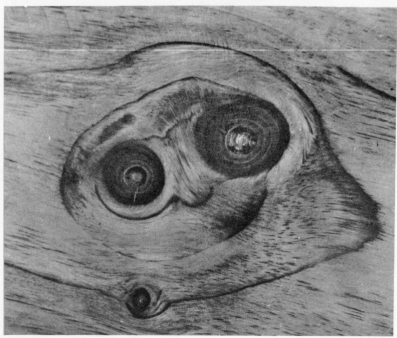

To the imaginative eye, Adirondack woodlands and wood offer startling resemblances. Here are examples: Top left and right show the same beech tree, snapped near an abandoned iron mine near Fort Ann in Washington County. Natural scars created a face which seemingly stares at one from all angles! At left, this unusual face (a smiling owl, perhaps?) was disclosed when the author found an old plank at a deserted lumber camp at Perkins Clearing, near Speculator. Planing and sandpapering it down brought out the happy face.

Stories in stone abound in the North Country. For instance, iron ore has been extracted since the Revolution from the Mineville and Port Henry areas. The Republic Steel Company mines at Mineville have been closed for some time, but this was a scene snapped 3,500 feet below the surface by the author, showing two miners drilling deeply into the ore-rich rock, preparatory to blasting. It was in an abandoned shaft in the Mineville area that the body of Susan Petz was found. (See chapter, "Diary of a Manhunt," page 20.)

Ore from this general area was mined, processed at Fort Edward, and eventually made into plates for the Union ironclad, the Monitor, at Troy. The Monitor hull has been located off Cape Hatteras, where the "cheesebox on a raft" capsized in a storm.

The Adirondacks are rich in minerals. For instance, talc, a soft mineral, is mined in St. Lawrence County; above is a photo taken in a shaft of the International Talc Company, considered in the 1960's as one of the world's biggest producers. The mineral is used in manufacture of paints, roofing, ceramics, rubber, textiles and insecticides. The area has been mined for decades.

At left is what is known as a "Herkimer Diamond." In actuality, it is a quartz crystal, found in Herkimer County. An excellent collection of such crystals, gathered by Clarence VanderVeer of Glenville, Schenectady County, is in the Museum of Natural History in New York. This piece is from his collection.

This unusual carving on a rock along Route 73, overlooking Upper Cascade Lake, is another "story in stone" in the North Country. At one time a stagecoach line ran through the "pass" to Lake Placid. In road maintenance during the 1930's, the crew found a large rock which had slipped off the side of Pitch-Off Mountain. It was decided to keep the rock in a small drive-off area, and to create a monument to the stagecoach days. Donald Rogers, Highway Department District Engineer, checked with Bill Petty, District Director of Lands and Forests (the rock was on State land) and later Rogers contacted Fred Carnes, owner of the Carnes Granite Co. of Au Sable Forks.

Lewis Brown of Chazy drew the sketch and Wilfred Carnes, using the region's first portable sandblasting machine, did the carving. It is best visible when the rock is wet.

When one travels through the North Country, it is possible to see evidences of the total disregard shown in creating reservoirs — most of them known as lakes today. Here are two prime examples. At left is a scene taken some years ago along the shore of *Cranberry Lake* in the northwestern mountain area. What you see are logs and stumps washed upon the shore, physical evidence that in the creation of the lake as we know it today crews did not bother to first clear the land. The dam holding back the Oswegatchie River was built in 1867, increased the lake from five surface square miles to eleven. Stumps still are buried beneath the surface. The reservoir was created for lumbering and power operations.

Lower photo shows *Indian Lake*, another body of water made larger by a dam, built in 1845, then rebuilt in 1898, to "control" the Hudson River. When water is drawn off, this desolate scene appears.

Unlike Cranberry Lake and Indian Lake, when the giant Sacandaga Reservoir was created in 1930 to relieve flooding of such cities as Albany by a rampaging Hudson, care was used to clear the area to be encompassed by the new basin. The Sacandaga is 29 miles long, with a surface area of about 42 square miles, and is controlled by the Hudson River-Black River Regulating Board.

Top is one area cleared of all save utility poles; these were eventually dragged out. Bottom shows homes that were evacuated and demolished at Batchellerville; note bridge construction. Larry Hart, Schenectady County Historian, has published an excellent book on the creation of the Sacandaga Reservoir.

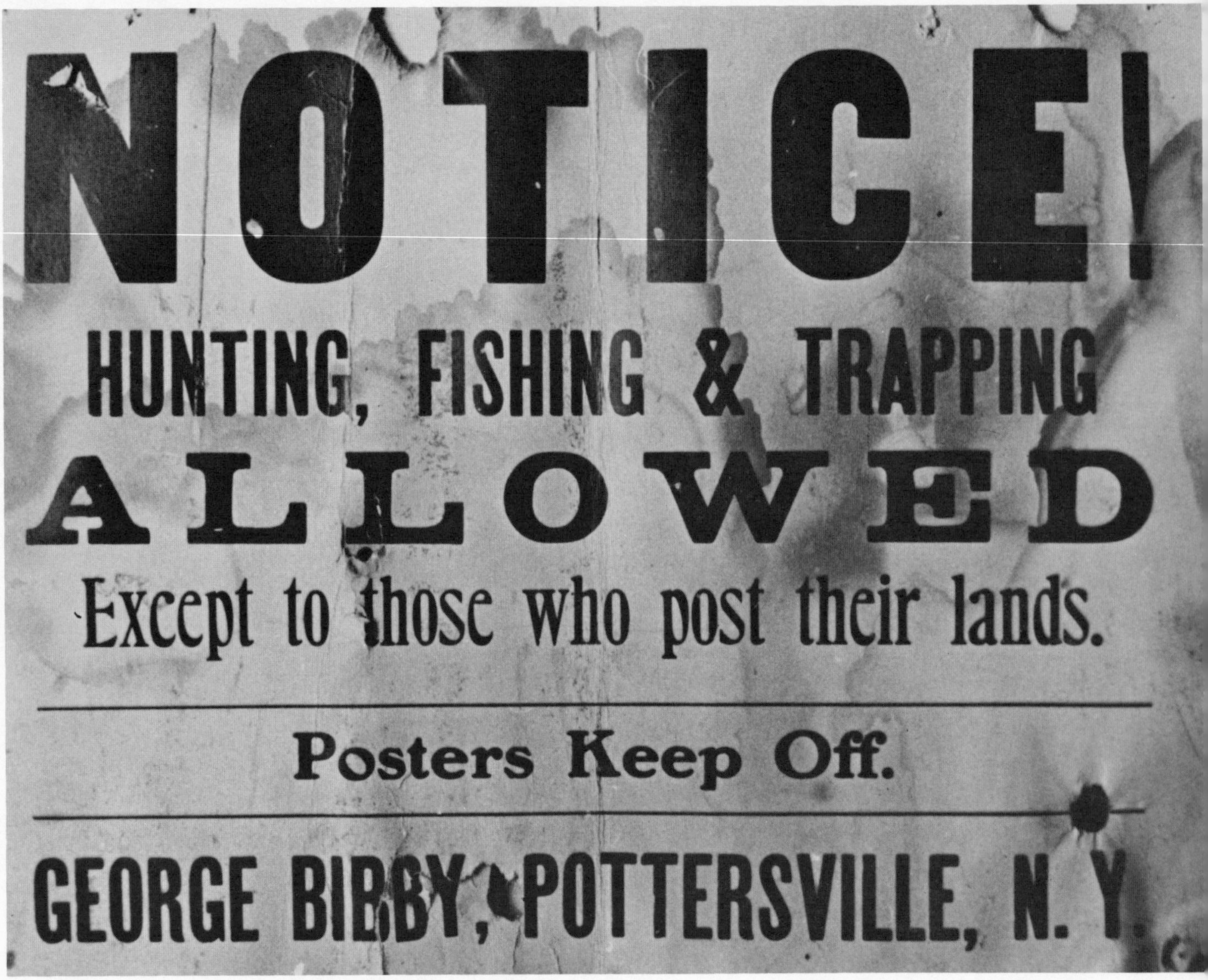

NOTICE!
HUNTING, FISHING & TRAPPING
ALLOWED
Except to those who post their lands.

Posters Keep Off.

GEORGE BIBBY, POTTERSVILLE, N. Y.

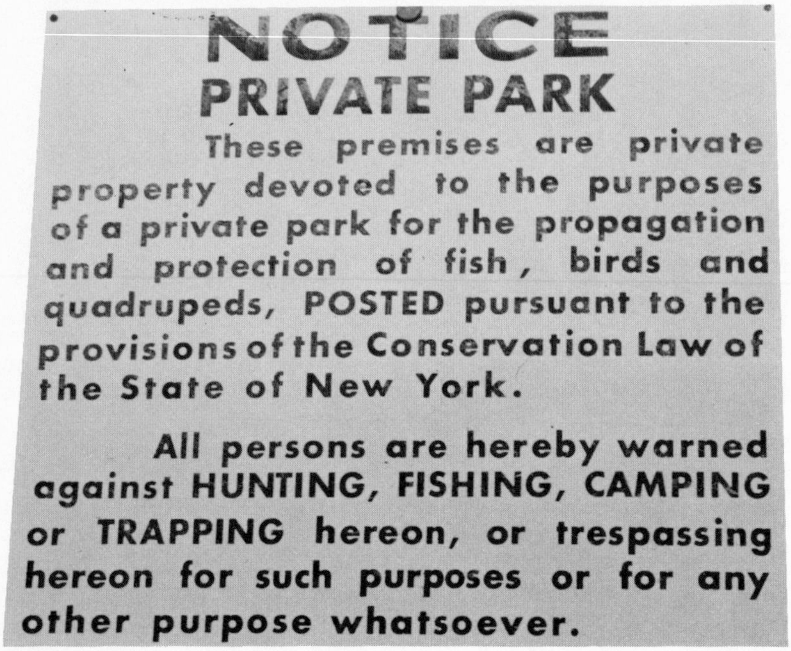

NOTICE
PRIVATE PARK

These premises are private property devoted to the purposes of a private park for the propagation and protection of fish, birds and quadrupeds, POSTED pursuant to the provisions of the Conservation Law of the State of New York.

All persons are hereby warned against HUNTING, FISHING, CAMPING or TRAPPING hereon, or trespassing hereon for such purposes or for any other purpose whatsoever.

Still another contrast of the North Country. Paul Crear of Severance furnished the author with the unusual "trespassing allowed" sign above. And at left is a type of sign becoming more common – no trespassing whatsoever. The sign above was posted some years ago; the sign at the left exists today. Such are becoming of concern to many, who see restrictions steadily compressing old hunting and fishing grounds. Note that while the land is posted as a game refuge, even hikers are prohibited.

As explained in the chapter on "Adirondack Wildlife," page 63, European boars were "stocked" in the Indian Lake area of Hamilton County by person or persons unknown. They were shot or captured; ones taken alive are in the Bronx Zoo in New York. Above is one of the shoats killed by irate Adirondackers who took matters into their own hands when the wild pigs began eating and rooting in their vegetable gardens.

Left: The last elk shot in the Adirondacks; date 1946. Hunter was astounded at first at the size of the huge "deer" he had taken. Head hangs in the Department of Environmental Conservation office at Warrensburg.

Ski touring, now a fast growing sport, has been enjoyed for years. In this scene a skier glides down a small incline on the trail out of T-Lake near Piseco; he and members of his group had visited T-Lake Falls. In some areas snow depth had reached 14 feet! Ski touring is probably most dramatized annually in the Rogers Rangers competition, during which skiers travel the entire length of Lake George.

The "personality," or "character" type seems to be vanishing from the Adirondack scene. Few persons offered better photographic possibilities than Noah John Rondeau the hermit, or Jacques Suzanne, the wolf breeder and tamer. But Archie "Bobcat" Rannie, who lived in the Bakers Mills section, matched them both. Rannie termed himself a hermit, but this has been denied by his neighbors. Admittedly, however, he was a distinct personality, a retired printer who took to the wilderness area to live in his own primitive way. He cooked porcupine as few others could. And he was the star of several local sportsmen's shows. He was, to put it mildly, a most unusual man.

The author would be totally remiss if he did not express deep appreciation to the memory of the late Walter J. Schoonmaker, above, an extraordinarily fine photographer, zoologist and artist. Walt has passed away, but left one of the finest collections of photographs, now in possession of this writer. Some of them have been used, with credit given.

"Schoonie," as he was sometimes called, studied vertebrate zoology at Cornell University and art at Syracuse and the University of Valencia, Spain. During his 35 years on the professional staff of the New York State Museum in Albany, he served first as assistant state zoologist and later as museum exhibit planner. He retired in 1958 to devote full time to his broad spectrum of talents and interest, wildlife photography and natural history writing, painting, drawing and lecturing.

He has had in his lifetime more than 3,000 of his wildlife photographs published and throughout his career has presented more than 1,000 illustrated lectures.

I do and shall miss this remarkable, this extraordinary man. Upon my death, his collection of negatives shall pass to the Museum of Natural History in New York, an organization which has requested them.

As Bill Roden said in his preface, the author is not partial to snowmobiles. However in 1973 he did relent and for the first time rode one of the machines — for $1 a foot, proceeds going to the Essex County Cancer Crusade. The author's father, a professional wrestler, died at age 42 of the disease. Above is the start of the ride — which raised more than $2,000, and, incidentally, tied up traffic around Tommy Brown's Restaurant at Lewis, where the event was held.

Left: Snowmobiling is now such a controversial sport that radio talk shows are based upon its aspects. Here the author appears on the popular Steve Fitz show.
Steve is at left.

197

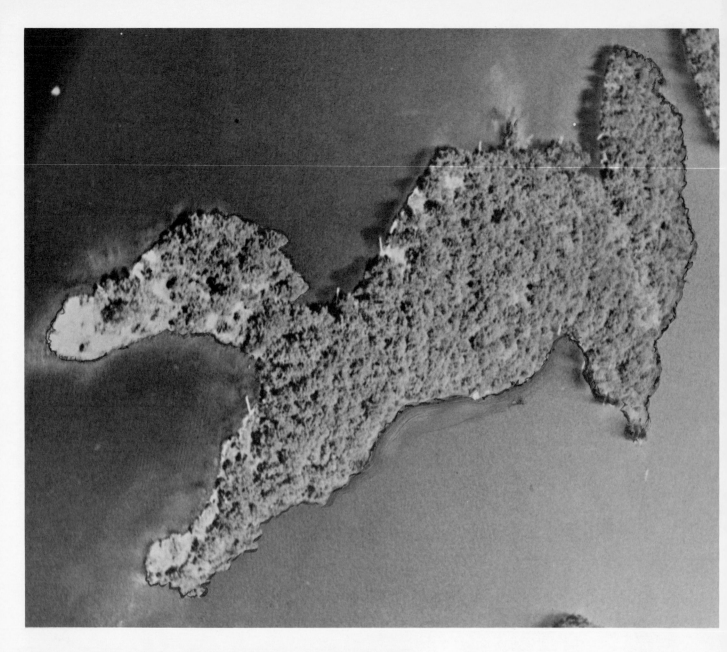

Both from the air and on the ground the unusual continues to present itself. Top: What looks like a poodle is in reality an island in Lake George. Left: Perhaps a half century or more ago a logger left his file in a tree crevice. The tree grew around it. It appeared later in a pulp log delivered to the West Virginia Pulp and Paper Mill at Mechanicville when that mill was in operation. Photo is by Tario Photo Service. Also found in pulp logs: Spent bullets. At Indian Lake lumberjacks found a tree with a horseshoe buried inside!

Perhaps it is fitting to end the pictorial portion of this volume with an illustration not of wildlife, not of the forest itself, but of a scene of tranquility at Elizabethtown. At left is the late and beloved Harry McDougal, "Mr. Republican" of Essex County, and a prime mover in matters of civic and historical interest. With him is Richard Lawrence, Jr., chairman of the Adirondack Park Agency, also a historian of note. Both men are standing near a dolphin fountain, of 1776 vintage, in the Colonial Garden at the historical museum in Elizabethtown. It is one of the finest areas of its kind in the nation and the public is welcomed.

ADDENDUM

After the capture of Robert Garrow, Sr., described in the chapter, "Diary of a Manhunt," Page 20, he was tried in County Court at Lake Pleasant, Hamilton County. He was found guilty of the murder of 18-year-old Philip Domblewski of Schenectady and sentenced to 25 years to life in Clinton Prison at Dannemora. During his stay on the witness stand, he testified to the killing of three other persons, Daniel Porter, 22, of Concord, Mass.; Alicia Hauck, 16, Syracuse, and Susan Petz, 21, of Skokie, Ill.

* * * * * * * * * *

The panther, Mac, pictured on Page 95, is dead. The animal became involved in an incident with a boy and was ordered caged; the boy was treated at Glens Falls Hospital and discharged. Mac was placed in a cage on orders of the Department of Environmental Conservation. In the cage next to him, at Animal Land, near Lake George, was his father. Unused to confinement, the panther went berserk, broke into his father's cage and the older mountain lion killed him in a savage brawl.

200